Praise for
Radical Trust

"Joe Healey validates the power of trust and the positive effect it has on organizational leadership. Certified public accounting firms and other professional service organizations and associations will benefit by implementing *Radical Trust,* especially with the millennium generation joining the workforce."

> —Albert E. Trexler, President and CEO
> Pennsylvania Institute of Certified Public Accountants

"The book offers accurate insights and instructions for those desiring to effectively lead their work force in today's highly competitive world. Through straight-talking practical advice, punctuated with practical examples, *Radical Trust* explains the critical function of how leaders gain people's confidence."

> —Glen A. Huff, Esq, President and Founder,
> Huff, Poole & Mahoney, P.C.

"The principles taught in this book create a culture that quickly responds to change and is rich in satisfaction. Implementing the recommendations of this book will help any leader. Joe Healey succinctly identifies leadership traits that build a unique and thriving culture of loyalty that provides results for both employees and customers. Our founder, Pam Nelson, who is featured in this book, is a great example of a leader whose sincerity and full engagement with our employees has created extraordinary performance."

> —Nina McCoy, President, CCG Systems, Inc.

"In *Radical Trust,* Joe Healey offers a practical yet fresh perspective on the impact employee trust in leadership has on gaining—a competitive edge. Joe uses insightful examples to model how to build trust that leads to engaged employees and, ultimately, unleashes the type of innovation that generates distinguishable differences in the market. Joe definitely hits the mark!"

> —Michael Brereton, President, Maritz Research

"It's wonderful! It is the most engrossing and fastest reading business book I've ever read. And as a librarian, I have read a lot of books. It is so relevant to building trust in our daily lives. I know what I am buying friends and family for Christmas presents."

> —Anne Lomax, retired librarian, Virginia Beach Public Libraries

"Healey brings to the forefront the importance of trust to business effectiveness in a new and fresh way. It takes the alignment of 'what we do,' 'what we say,' and 'who we are' to build trust with others. Business relationships founded on trust may be the single biggest employee retention tool available. Healey shows us how to build those kinds of relationships. Any leader would benefit from the insights he shares in *Radical Trust*."

> —Doug McMillon, President and CEO, Sam's Club

"Healey is right on target. His book is a clear explanation of how instilling loyalty in a company becomes the differentiator in building an extraordinary culture. Having the chance to experience the loyalty factor from both sides at CiCi's Pizza, mentored by Joe Croce (featured in this book) as his employee and now in my current role as the President, I know that the head of any organization will learn great lessons from Healey's work."

> —Craig Moore, President, CiCi's Pizza

"Healey shows an organization how to set itself apart with service excellence, financial success, and employee loyalty. For progressive leaders who seek a comprehensive how-to, this book provides not only the framework, but also the proof that it works. Even after twenty years of experience, I learned things that will provide invaluable assistance for many more to come."

> —Loriann Putzier, Principal and COO, IntegraCare Corporation

"*Radical Trust* is not a book of theory, but a hands-on, how-to book of practical ideas to help leaders establish the Radical Trust that will change their relationships, their workplaces, and ultimately, their lives. Buy this book if you want to be a long-lived, successful, and well-loved leader."

> —Barbara A. Glanz, author of *Handle with CARE: Motivating and Retaining Employees* and coauthor with Ken Blanchard of *The Simple Truths of Service*

"Healey's model is an invaluable tool for leaders who want to harness the forward momentum that trust can bring to an organization. This book captures and describes the role that trust plays as an intrinsic value that people of all ages, genders, and cultures must have with their leaders."

> —Genien Carlson, former first Vice-President, Mellon Bank

"*Radical Trust* is entertaining reading. Healey shares his insight through useful, real-life, everyday examples. Trust is the key building block of successful leadership, and this book is your blueprint."

> —Ronald L. Hrebinko, MD, Associate Professor, Urologic/ Surgical Oncology, University of Pittsburgh School of Medicine

RADICAL
TRUST

How Today's Great Leaders
Convert People to Partners

JOE HEALEY

BICENTENNIAL
1807
WILEY
2007
BICENTENNIAL

John Wiley & Sons, Inc.

Published by John Wiley & Sons, Inc., Hoboken, New Jersey.
Published simultaneously in Canada.

Wiley Bicentennial Logo: Richard J. Pacifico

For general information on our other products and services or for technical support, please
contact our Customer Care Department within the United States at (800) 762-2974, outside
the United States at (317) 572-3993 or fax (317) 572-4002.

Wiley also publishes its books in a variety of electronic formats. Some content that appears in
print may not be available in electronic books. For more information about Wiley products,
visit our web site at www.wiley.com.

Library of Congress Cataloging-in-Publication Data:

Healey, Joe, 1959–
   Radical trust : how today's great leaders convert people to partners / Joe Healey.
     p. cm.
   ISBN 978-0-470-12832-9 (cloth)
   1. Trust. 2. Employees—Attitudes. 3. Leadership. 4. Organizational
behavior. I. Title.
   HF5548.8.H366 2007
   658.4'092—dc22

               2007008871

Printed in the United States of America.

10 9 8 7 6 5 4 3 2 1

To Jill
My wonderful life partner in whom
I have Radical Trust. We have shared the great joy
that is derived from trust in a relationship and how
much is possible because of it!

To Betts and Joe
My dear mother and father whose encouragement
has always meant the world to me. I have trusted
you to always be there.

To Joe III, Jen, and Josh
You have allowed me to grow as a parent
and are now my trusted companions.

Contents

Part III
Character Trust *(Who You Are)*

Part IV
Communication Trust *(What You Say)*

Part V
Loyalty Trust *(How They Feel)*

Acknowledgments

A heartfelt thank you to the following people for advancing the ideas of this book:

- Sam Horn, author of *Pop, Stand Out in Any Crowd,* who teased out the title.
- John Blumberg, author of *Silent Alarm* for his wise thoughts on character.
- John Putzier, author of *Get Weird, 101 Innovative Ways to Make Your Company a Great Place to Work,* who meticulously critiqued an early draft.
- Beth Lira, my sister, a great leader in her own right, who greatly influenced my work.
- Barbara Glanz, author of *Contagious Enthusiasm,* and Steve Shapiro, author of *Goal Free Living,* for their early guidance about choosing a publisher.
- Kim Cannon, director of human resources at the Society of Automotive Engineers, who gave early confirmation of the validity of this book's unique approach.

- Nina McCoy, president of CCG Systems, who validated the idea of making the power of relationships a central theme of this book.
- Jill's family and my family for their encouragement and excitement over the cover design.
- My neighborhood buddies: the Sweenys, Clements, Oliviers, and Allards, who were a rich source of encouragement for this project.
- Meg La Borde and Clint Greenleaf, brilliant publishing executives who were a great source of advice.
- My first bosses, over 25 years ago, in banking who set a standard for what a leader and mentor should be; thanks to David Leach, Mindy Englemeier, and Genien Carlson.
- Matt Holt, my editor, and his team, Shannon Vargo and Jessica Campilango, at John Wiley & Sons, Inc., who were terrific partners.
- Kim Dayman and her team in marketing and design at Wiley, who created a fantastic cover.
- Paul McCarthy who captured us with his clever illustration.
- Matthew Land and the staff at Publications Development Company, whose editing and production expertise greatly sharpened this work.

Preface

During my 25-plus years as a banker, entrepreneur, chief executive, consultant, and speaker, I have had the privilege to lead my own organizations and to be exposed to the inside workings of countless others and their leaders. In that time, I have seen several important factors that drive success and failure. But no factor has stood so tall or stooped so low as *trust* to impact success. Managers who are capable of building high trust dramatically increase their ability to lead, to create loyalty, to retain talent, and to foster creativity. Conversely, I have seen extraordinarily talented people greatly reduce their success because they are not good at building trust.

Trust has always been important. But the early years of the twenty-first century have revealed a significant shift in what it takes to be successful. Capital, followed by information, was the key to success in the twentieth century. However, we have moved beyond the Industrial Age through the Information Age to what I call the *Age of Talent*. The need for talent is being driven by economic factors that will continue to affect the way we do business for decades into this third millennium.

For example, tech-savvy consumers and the globalization of business are driving greater competition. This is forcing organizations to innovate, which requires more talented employees. Employees of developed countries have far more freedom today than ever before, economically and socially, to choose the job and boss they like.

In fact, as you will see, the greater freedom to make economic choices is causing younger generations to be very intolerant of bad bosses. Many misconstrue this as a poor work ethic, when in reality it is a sign that old management practices are not adapting to today's market conditions that demand more trust. Therefore, whether you are managing generation X, Y, or boomer; black, Hispanic, or white; in India, Europe, or the United States; the economic value resulting from building trust is simple: Talented people are more productive and tend to stay around longer if they have bosses they can trust.

In addition, to remain competitive, we are seeing massive changes in the way companies do business. We will continue to see organizations evolve and change well into the first half of the twenty-first century. High trust increases the pace or speed of change and low trust slows down the implementation of plans, initiatives, and new processes. The cost of low trust is greater resistance to change, a higher cost of change, and far more burnout. One of the primary benefits of this book is to teach managers how to build the kind of trust that ensures success in managing and accelerating change.

This book is a practical guide to aid you in building and sustaining a unique, even radical, level of trust that will grease the skids for your talents to emerge and your employees' talents to flourish. Using case studies from four leaders who have created Radical Trust in their personal and professional lives, I will show you that the competencies these leaders used to build trust have made them rich in all senses of the word. Although this book is focused on building trust at work, these trust-building concepts are just as relevant to your personal life.

I am one of very few consultants or speakers who has been teaching trust as a central part of leadership over the past 20 years. Recently, the topic has switched from being a *moral choice* of more upstanding leaders to an *economic necessity* in the way managers lead. This book is unique because it does not use the majority of the content to tell you why. There is only one chapter devoted to the why question: Chapter 2, "The Business Case for Trust." This book invests 90 percent of its content in focusing on the more practical *how* to build trust. This is the only book on trust that fully focuses on in-depth case studies on what works in the real world.

Three Reasons to Read This Book

This book will help you become more successful as a manager by harnessing the powerful force of trust. When managers have high trust, they are more fulfilled, have more fun, and therefore contribute more. However, building trust in the midst of conflicting demands, limited resources, and competing loyalties can be daunting. This book provides a practical road map.

You will learn from highly successful leaders in some of the toughest business sectors who successfully struggled with today's low-trust world to build high-trust relationships. These leaders will teach you how to avoid the stressful duality that often develops as you gain more and more responsibility. You don't have to choose between people and the bottom line. Radical Trust leaders build both the bottom line and people. The four competencies that enable you to cultivate Radical Trust act as a powerful force to create exceptional results at work and home during good times and tough times.

The second reason to read this book is that developing the four competencies to build Radical Trust makes great business sense. You need results and you know that low trust marginalizes cooperation, buy-in, and execution. In addition, like so many managers, you may be exasperated and exhausted by the petty games, negative conflict, and backstabbing that washes over an organization when trust is low.

Currently, organizations spend many of their resources on initiatives that are stifled or doomed by a lack of trust. The following are examples of just a few of the many business initiatives that benefit from higher trust:

- Increase creativity and knowledge transfer.
- Increase internal collaboration that reduces silos, departmental barriers, and turf wars.

- Increase the ability to recruit and retain various generations of talent.
- Increase the capacity of people to move past generational and diversity issues to establish productive connections and communication.
- Increase the competency of employees to improve service, embrace change, and manage conflict. This is sometimes referred to as increasing the emotional quotient (EQ).
- Increase partnerships with vendors to create cost-effective outsourcing solutions.

Trust is central to all these initiatives. Think about it. If you have low trust, you can guarantee that all of these initiatives will be stunted. In fact, you will learn that these four Radical Trust competencies are the real answers to your "people" problems. For example, people are delighted to find that mastering these competencies provides the key to resolving generational differences and is the most essential element in raising the emotional quotient of your managers and employees.

There are many indicators that show why the ideas in this book have become so important to you and your organization. Media attention spotlighted the business scandals that plagued the beginning of the twenty-first century. Those companies paid a heavy price for their breach of trust, and the media continues to cover story after story of businesses and bosses that breach trust because the public consciousness has shifted to a far less tolerant view of weak trust. Government regulation, consumer vigilance, and lack of employee loyalty all show that people are exercising their ability to vote with their checkbooks and career choices. Employee surveys have shown repeatedly that employees are concerned about the cost of low trust.

The third reason to read this book is that the high-trust success of the leaders in this book provides a practical set of lessons to teach the competencies that produce profit and great relationships. It is not a parable, so it does not use fictitious, unrealistic examples. It is more inspiring than fiction because life is far better than fiction, and because these are real people, you will find their successes easy to duplicate.

Authentic Case Studies

I have resisted the common trend to use celebrity leaders who have name recognition but little connection to your reality as examples. My examples are of people whose behaviors and lives you can respect. The case studies are the result of relationships generated by my years as a banker, businessperson, and speaker/consultant. I focus particularly on four leaders whose successful careers serve as a model of how trust maximizes performance and personal satisfaction. Here is a quick introduction to the four Radical Trust leaders central to this book:

1. Pam Nelson, CEO of CCG Systems, built a thriving technology firm. She created one of the most extraordinary partnerships in the daunting technology sector between customers, employees, and vendors. She recently sold her company to her employees. Pam's employees see her as a tough and savvy businesswoman. They say, "She is like a drug: After spending time with her, we are on a high."

2. Joe Croce is the founder and former CEO of the rapidly growing 600-plus restaurant chain, CiCi's Pizza. This restaurant entrepreneur created handsome profits for his franchisees and himself in spite of operating on razor-thin margins and managing the constant change driven by their growth. At a recent franchise meeting where Joe announced the sale of the company to employees, hard-bitten, multiunit-restaurant owners shed tears as they went in front of an open microphone to express their gratitude to him.

3. Harry Young, producer and television executive, used his production genius to found an international nonprofit youth development organization, YES, that is reshaping the way traditional institutions like YMCA's and Boys & Girls Clubs use media to reach youth. He is one of the key executives who built the successful Family Channel. Harry is an extraordinary person whose

leadership has built an organization with international reach that has protected and supported the success of young people who may not otherwise have even lived beyond their youth. The lessons he shares about building trust in the midst of broken trust are very relevant to the corporate landscape of today.

4. Steve Krajenka's ability to build trust translated into the highest grossing sales zone of the world's second largest clothing retailer, the GAP. Over a billion dollars in sales were generated by his high-trust team that managed over 9,000 employees, and 335 stores. They successfully coped with multiple generations in a highly creative fashion-driven business that normally has extremely high turnover and burnout. When he decided to take two years off to spend time with his wife and teenage sons, Gap managers created a book espousing his management principles and inspiration.

These leaders and their organizations have either been clients of mine or I have served on their board. I have seen up close the validity and power of their lessons. As their stories reveal, they have mastered trust in such a deep way that they have created exceptional bottom-line successes. Past and present employees trust them deeply and even revere them.

I have also included examples from other clients and experiences from my banking career, my role as a chief executive, and various consulting projects. My commitment in this book is to share these important principles about building trust from an authentic and practical perspective.

In summary, people who develop Radical Trust get more done in business and enjoy much richer personal relationships, which translates into greater prosperity and fulfillment. Just like money, trust is something people want in abundance; but, like building monetary wealth, building trust is complex. This book takes a critical component of leadership that is also a complex relationship issue and breaks it down into four practical competencies and shows you how to master each so that you accumulate the kind of trust that produces radical results.

PART I

Trust:
Your Most Important Competitive Weapon

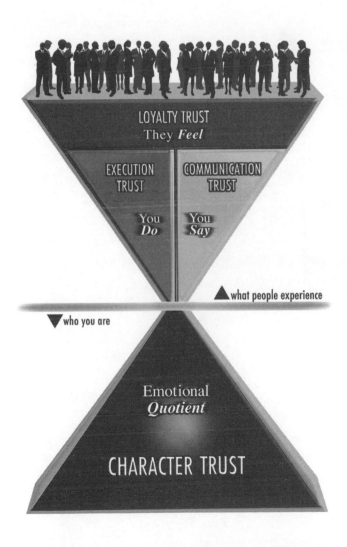

1

Discovering the Power of Trust

Eighteen years ago, I was standing among the vending machines, microwaves, and cigarette smoke of the break room of a manufacturing plant saying goodbye to numerous employees. George, a dapper, 45-year-old informal leader of the plant approached me to deliver a message that was one of my great life lessons. George spoke very deliberately with his Alabama drawl. He extended his hand and grasped mine firmly and warmly to say goodbye. I had just ended a one-year consulting deal to turn this company around and this was farewell.

A year prior, I had signed a contract that gave me an ownership stake and the title of general manager. An average labor cost of 19 percent of revenues was draining this 48-store retail and manufacturing business of its profits. Labor cost should have been 14 percent and that would have represented a good margin for that industry. In the span of that year, we managed to get the labor cost down to our target of 14 percent and my work there was finished.

Because of George's wisdom and the respect he had from everyone in this organization, he was a key person whom I relied on for advice. We had been through a lot of crazy times. We negotiated with the bank that was trying to pull our several hundred thousand dollar line of credit which would have thrown us into bankruptcy. We made significant changes to workflows and processes. We consolidated a few of our operations. We struggled with the low morale that resulted from stagnant wages. And we made some tough personnel changes to fix quality problems. Although, my most memorable moment was a crisis at our main plant that forced George to go looking for two missing managers, who were rumored to be having an affair. George laughed as he revealed his awkward discovery of these managers in the two-story underground high-security vault. George's status as a highly respected manager was instrumental to us forging cooperation related to many change initiatives.

With my hand in his callused, enveloping one, George said, "Joe, you are a communicator." Feeling flattered but not sure what he meant, I said, "Thank you, why do you say that?" He then surprised me by saying, "You know your plan is not the reason this company got turned around. You were the fourth consultant we had in four years and your plan was no better than theirs." Now this was not something a departing consultant wanted to hear on his way out the door. I would have liked to believe that my strategies were central to our success. So with great interest, I listened as George continued.

George then said with a tone of finality (these are not his exact words but I think they are pretty close), "Joe, you know we have all been very afraid here for years with all the cutbacks, wage freezes, and numerous consultants coming in here—each with some new fangled cost-cutting plan. We were tired and no one trusted anyone else. That changed this past year."

My concern at my plan not being so valuable in George's eyes faded quickly as my eyes teared up. He was giving me some credit for people there having stronger relationships. George went on to say again, "You took time to talk to us, not at us." Then he said something that really touched my heart, "You made us feel you were with us, one of us."

As I went on to other consulting assignments, I often pondered George's words. And I realized that he had pointed out something that was quite accidental. I don't think I would have purposefully repeated it in other endeavors if he had not brought it to my attention.

During this consulting assignment, something different happened related to my sensitivity about our employees. This retail chain, which had its own manufacturing facilities, had its largest plant in a very poor section of Cincinnati, Ohio. I was deeply moved by the plight of several of the plant workers. They were working in a hot environment doing very repetitive work, standing on their feet all day. I became more familiar than I ever thought I would be with the cost of, among other things, alcohol and drug abuse.

Over the years, this company had many success stories of people who turned their lives around and who expressed openly that their job at this company was a big reason for this. All the employees knew the owner and many had high loyalty toward him. He was the grandson of the founder. They affectionately called him by his first name, Jim. Those who knew him when he was just a kid visiting his grandfather's business still called him Jimmy.

I was emotionally touched by the lot of many of these employees and the loyalty that Jim had from his people made me want to earn that same thing. At this company, I had a high level of compassion that drove a deep desire to partner with these people, to respect them, and to see them succeed. You see, sadly, as my wife Jill would tell you, I had become like many entrepreneurs or corporate managers: very good at getting results or, what in modern terms we call, execution. That's why Jim hired me.

However, on this consulting assignment, I was more invested in the people. But I did not realize how that affected the success of our work until George's comment. In fact, George's comment coincided with another unique feeling that I had as I packed up my office and prepared to say my goodbyes. I was much more choked up than I had been before and was caught off guard by it. I was going to miss these people: both the ones I enjoyed and even the pain-in-the-butt people, of which we had no shortage. My valuing my employees permitted me to have a much more effective relationship with them, which translated into tangible loyalty toward each other.

This was long before the time that change was considered a business topic or that *change management* was even used as a routine term. Nevertheless, it was clear that I was learning about the connection between trust and leading change. My stumbling into this key trust-building competency was driven by my heart or emotions. Much of what I say in this book will appeal to your left brain or analytical side. But make no mistake, I hope to impact your heart and how you think about the people you serve. The case studies will prove that having a heart for your people and your customers is critical to success.

George's message shed light on something important that had happened to me and made me want to duplicate it at my next endeavor. This message was the first in a series of lessons that have brought me to the findings I am sharing with you in this book. There was much more I had yet to learn about building trust in the midst of change and hard times. But this experience taught me that while strategy and innovation may be important, success comes much faster when you create a platform of trust on which people can stand and build.

This leads me to the next chapter. If you study history, you will conclude that in the past, management did not need to care as much about people or trust as it does today. However, the climate has changed and there is ample evidence that to be trusted by our employees, customers, investors, vendors, and community is a very important business objective. Before I go into more depth on the four competencies to build trust and the inspiring and practical examples of my four case studies, here is the business case for trust.

2

The Business Case for Trust

While working with a client recently, I discovered an allegory to describe the impact of trust. This client was feeling the pain of rapid growth. The stress of the growth uncovered low trust between some managers and their employees. However, there were several other managers and teams who had contrastingly high trust between them. The difference in the performance between the low-trust groups and the high-trust groups was like the difference between analog dial-up, and digital, broadband Internet access. The low-trust group who were like analog dial-up had far less bandwidth for change and innovation and were much slower at everything.

Trust is something that can be built and, like digital technology, can create profound improvements in productivity. So, a strong case can be made for the need to master those competencies that build trust. In this chapter, I provide data that proves the financial success that Radical Trust leadership has garnered for organizations and individuals. I will also reveal the economic trends and cultural changes that make building and sustaining trust much more important and urgent today than it was in the past.

Digital technology was embraced as critical to business success as a result of the convergence of several factors. And so it is with trust. Business realities are establishing the need for trust not only to be a critical management competency today, but also for many decades to come.

Proof: Radical Trust Creates Radical Success

The four primary leaders and their organizations who are profiled in this book prove that Radical Trust is a critical weapon in competitive markets that enables managers to lead an organization to great financial results as well as creating an organization people love. Here are both factual data and anecdotal testimony to prove it.

Radical Trust Leader 1: Joe Croce

Position: Founder and former CEO, CiCi's Pizza, a 600-store franchise chain.

Proof of Financial Success: CiCi's Pizza has 600 restaurants in 27 states. In January 2007, *Entrepreneur* magazine ranked them number one in the Italian restaurant franchises category. In 2006, *Restaurants & Institutions* magazine named them Best in Value in its Annual Consumer Choice Survey in the pizza category. In 2005, the *Wall Street Journal* named CiCi's one of the Top 25 Franchises. In 2004 and 2005, the *Nation's Restaurant News* ranked CiCi's as number one for sales and unit growth in the pizza chain category. The founder, Joe Croce, retired three years ago at the age of forty-four and left behind numerous millionaires he helped to create. Some are now employee owners and some franchise owners.

Proof of Radical Trust: Craig Moore was mentored by Joe and was part of the team that bought CiCi's and replaced Joe as president. He tells us:

> When I came to CiCi's 15 years ago and met with Joe Croce, he (like all before) painted a picture for a great personal future if there were results that he expected. In past companies and positions, the painted picture was not real and when results were attained, there was always some "company" reason or other half-baked excuse why the promises were stalled or not available at all. I learned early on with Joe that not only would he follow through on his promises, he often would do it at his own detriment. There were many years in the early days that the lieutenants would prosper at Joe's expense. He lived modestly so he could proceed to build the team that he thought would get him to his ultimate goals (while all lieutenants exceeded their personal goals).
>
> As one manager told us, "If you were good enough to play on Joe's team and then make the cut day in and day out, the benefits kept coming in. Joe built loyalty by exceeding our expectations with personal growth that equated to financial gain. It was never about the money for the ones that stayed at CiCi's. It was about being on the team and hitting the goals. And when we did, the things that were promised happened every time. We always knew that if Joe Croce said that he was going to do something, it was going to happen. If you learned this early in your career with CiCi's, the tough love was easy to take. Joe was consistent with his tough style. He cared about our success and only wanted those who would sacrifice for the team. He ended up on top and left behind a wildly successful future for those who played on his team."
>
> A plaque that was mounted at the entrance to CiCi's corporate headquarters by one of Joe's successors reads: "This building is dedicated to Joe Croce. May the passion, pride, and high ethical standards upon which you founded these companies never falter!"

Radical Trust Leader 2: Steve Krajenka

Position: Zone vice president, GAP
Proof of Financial Success: In 2004, within one-year of Steve's tenure as zone vice president, his became the highest grossing sales zone of the world's second largest clothing retailer, the GAP. Over $1 billion in sales were generated by his high-trust team that managed over 9,000 employees and 335 stores.
Proof of Radical Trust: The following is one of 50 testimonials written by employees when Steve went on sabbatical to spend time with his wife and teenage boys:

> I do want you to know that I am so happy to have met, and worked with someone that holds the same values as myself and was able to lead a successful team. I know that everyone here feels that they had an important part in making this brand successful, and that was because of your great leadership. How many leaders do you know who make their employees like going to work? And, how many leaders do you know who let people know that there is more to life than work? These are two questions that I will always remember because of you, and are qualities that I will always look for in a leader.
>
>   Rosie Munoz, Office Administrator

Radical Trust Leader 3: Pam Nelson

Position: CEO, CCG Systems, The company's "Faster" software provides fleet management solutions.
Proof of Financial Success: Pam and her team took a small tech start-up on the verge of failing and increased sales from $150,000 to $3.8 million. She just sold her company to her employees through an employee stock option plan, and Pam's 29 original employees/partners are now becoming employee owners.

Proof of Radical Trust: Rick D. Longobart is the fleet services superintendent for the city of Inglewood and his statement that follows is one of many examples of the Radical Trust that Pam has with her customers:

> I first met Pam in the summer of 1994 while installing a new fleet management software system, at which time I was just entering my supervisory career. Being a new supervisor, it was important to me to impress people using my expertise, knowledge, and managerial skills. However, Pam was not impressed with my ability to direct staff and demonstrate my autocratic approaches. The reason Pam was not impressed with this style of management is Pam's belief system is not based on instructing staff to complete work on a hierarchy level of management. Instead, her approach is to implement change based on the total quality management leadership approach. Her approaches are actually simple solutions that most of us overlook.
>
> While most of us attempt to invoke change by telling people how or what to be, Pam actually uses the concept of self-empowerment by listening to one's concerns, needs, and purpose in life to bring out their strong points. Pam has been very successful because she knows that you can be more effective by leading by example than by telling people what to do. She uses the following approach. The difference between a leader and a boss: The leader leads, and the boss drives. Over the years, Pam has been my mentor, because I have found that these examples are effective . . . I too have adopted her leadership style and it has made me a successful leader.

Radical Trust Leader 4: Harry Young

Position: Former film and TV producer; founder YES (Youth Entertainment Studios): A nonprofit organization that provides solutions for at-risk youth.

Proof of Success: Because this organization is focused on changing lives and not monetary profit, I will use this leader's prior success in business to demonstrate the profitability of his Radical Trust practices: As vice president of original programming for the Family Channel and senior vice president of Family Productions Inc., Harry helped build a TV station and film company that were later sold to ABC for $3.2 billion. Harry then turned his sights on a greater vision of using media to help youth.

Proof of Radical Trust: Brian Toppins, 23, and Darrell Monroe, 23, who were participants in the YES program and are now volunteers had this to say: "It was nice to come to a place that was like home where you know a father figure will be there."

In spite of having YES studios all over America and in London, Harry remains active in a local pilot studio where he maintains his office. There he remains a father figure to the many teenagers who come through that facility's doors.

Derek Springs, a graduate of the YES program, says the following about Harry: "When I come to the studio, Harry is always there and I feel like I don't always have to watch my back. I feel safe there and Harry doesn't judge me. No matter what I have done, Harry makes me feel valuable."

Amiracle Freeman, a current YES participant, says: "I love Mr. Harry because he genuinely cares about young people."

These leaders are strong proof of the benefit of Radical Trust. Therefore, you may be tempted to skip the rest of this chapter because you are already convinced that there is a strong business case that makes trust critical to success. Please feel free to do so, but you may want to read what follows to get a sense of the magnitude of the shift that is making these trust competencies so important and creating such great opportunities for those who master them.

Trust Is Becoming a Necessity

Let me start this justification by focusing on your world. Take a moment to think about the highest performing group of people you have ever worked with—now or previously in your career. Do you have these people in your mind—stop and picture them. Then answer these questions: Did this group have high trust? What would have happened if trust were diminished in that group? I ask clients these questions all the time. Overwhelmingly, they say that trust, in fact, is the single biggest contributor to a high-performing team and agree that lack of trust is the single biggest reason for dysfunctions on teams.

You may be saying, "But wait a minute, Joe. Organizations have operated quite profitably throughout history while having very low trust between management and workers." It used to be no surprise to come across scores of managers who got the job done but their people could not trust them as far as they could throw them. In fact, you may have worked for one.

One reason low-trust managers and organizations were financially successful in the past is that most organizations were focused more on productivity as a function of keeping cost down. So their economics didn't demand the more complex work environment for which trust is essential. Today's competitive climate requires far more creativity, knowledge sharing, problem solving, and diverse talent.

That is why there is a sudden surge in the need for trust. Things have changed dramatically because of several economic factors. For example, low-cost production is not the singular issue it once was. For more than a decade, organizations have tried to compete globally by getting people to work harder and cheaper. However, organizations are realizing that, while hard work is important, working smart is really what they need employees to do. While managers who can instill fear can get people to work pretty hard, managers who can build trust get people to work harder and more creatively over the long run.

Therefore, most organizations have shifted from solely focusing on productivity to adding value by applying creativity. This has led to constantly improving processes. You have certainly seen that, in the past decade, change is the new norm. All this change requires far more communication. It also requires constant knowledge sharing.

Another big shift is that we can no longer tolerate large numbers of mediocre workers bogging down an organization. The need to develop talent and retain it is far more important than it was in the past.

Employees Are More Likely to Quit Low-Trust Bosses

The availability of information and the transient nature of the world make it very hard for organizations to hide bad management practices. Compared to workers in the Industrial Age, the economic wealth that the working world now enjoys is giving workers unprecedented power to quit their jobs and invest their talents elsewhere. Simply put, low-trust management did not cost as much during the Industrial Age and thus was more tolerated. The British comedian and star of the BBC comedy show, *Monty Python,* reveals how some workers feel about their bosses.

> *I find it rather easy to portray a businessman: Being bland, rather cruel, and incompetent comes naturally to me.*
> —*John Cleese (1939–)*

The reason low trust didn't cost as much during the Industrial Age is that employees had minimal ability to hold the bad manager accountable by quitting. The marketplace was not nearly as competitive. Today, the market holds managers accountable because customers press organizations for the level of service and quality that only higher functioning employees can provide.

High Trust Spurs Innovation and Profits

Let me give you two quick examples of how building trust pays off in today's market.

Google Trust

When Google started as an Internet search engine company, its competitors were providing search results that allowed those that paid for advertising to achieve higher rankings. Of course, this reduced the accuracy of the search result and was considered deceptive because in many cases the user was not made aware of which listings were a legitimate result of the search and which were showing up because money had changed hands.

Google opted to embrace a higher trust relationship with its users and would not let advertising income dictate its listings. Instead, it put a separate area to the right of the listing for paid advertiser's links that were relevant to the search. This section was clearly labeled: "Sponsored Links." One of Google's founders and one of three top leaders, Sergey Brin, was worth $14 billion in 2006 as a result of Google generated wealth. He underscored that Google would take a high-trust approach when he said we will "do no evil."

It is further interesting to note that Google was not first to market with its product. So it did not have the luxury of making easy money and high profits that then allowed them to take the higher ground. Google started on the higher ground because it *was* a competitive advantage. If you want some interesting reading, search the Web for "early search engines" and you will find that there were at least 24 search engines or directories that were competing between 1993 and 2006. Even though Google came on the scene rather late in 1998, it dominates today.

Cost of Broken Trust and the Power of Harnessing It

Employees of American Airlines would have agreed with John Cleese's snide statement had you talked to them after what they found out in 2003. American Airlines CEO Donald J. Carty asked rank and file employees to concede deep cuts in their compensation. However, he quietly got the board to approve giving senior executives perks and bonuses. He acted under the misguided belief that they needed to secretly do this to retain top talent, but could not be honest with the airline employees who were taking pay cuts.

By law, Carty had to make these executive perks public in a filing to the Securities and Exchange Commission (SEC). So he waited until the day after the union agreed to take massive wage cuts and then made the SEC filing that told the public about the executive perks. The union members felt betrayed and threatened a revote because of his bad faith.

In the past century, an executive may have gotten away with this low-trust tactic. However, in this case, the board asked Carty to resign rather than risk the union reneging on its vote to cut wages.

With a painful lesson learned by American Airlines management, a new age had dawned and this story had a good ending. Wade Goodwyn of National Public Radio told a different story about the company on December 7, 2006, that revealed the power of trust to create results.

American Airlines Vice President Carmine J. Romano, who is in charge of American Airline's maintenance facility, broke from the old tradition to protect his power. He began to share power and decision making with the union in an attempt to spur innovation and cost cutting. The union willingly cut their wages as he built trust. Employees were given input into running the operation.

Dennis Burchette, president of TWU Local 514, spoke of the dramatic difference trust makes in permitting people to grow, change, and innovate when he said, "When I have my union meetings now and I've got 200 guys in there, instead of complaining about management, they sound like businesspeople. . . . Look what they're doing to us. They're changing us down here. We used to cuss management and now all we do is talk about business."

The airlines and the union developed a shared goal. Instead of giving in to the global trend to farm out costly labor-intensive work like airline maintenance to cheaper labor markets, they set out to improve their operation to be able to compete. They were so successful that they not only avoided the job losses associated with outsourcing, but began to "in-source" work from overseas. The workers redesigned entire business models. It used to take 800 mechanics working 25 days to perform an overhaul. Now, it is accomplished with 450 mechanics working 13 days. The over-all cost was reduced by 55 percent.

Romano summarizes their success with a simple statement, "When they implement, it is a much quicker success." The business case for trust is solidly made by the fact that American Airlines has become so good at maintenance that they moved beyond servicing their own planes and now have 50 outside customers. They estimate that revenue from in-sourcing in 2007 will be $100 million and in 2008 will be $175 million.

Employee Partnership and Collaboration

Global competition is forcing people and organizations to embrace the idea of partnership with customers, employees, and even vendors.

Organizations are waking up to the fact that if the only thing at the center of the business relationship is wage, salary, commission, fee, price, margin, and/or volume, then you are not a partner adding value and you become extremely vulnerable to low-cost competitors. It is the same with people. A person's value is not based on how cheaply he or she will work. A person's economic value is based on the combination of knowledge-capital, skills, and ability to team with others to make contributions. If an employer can't trust you to partner with a team member to deliver, all your degrees and experience are worth very little.

This works the same way for an employer. How much an organization pays is no longer the exclusive measure of the value of a job. For example, employee surveys have been telling us for years that money is not the only currency that retains talent. Money used to be the most dominant reason people left a job. People now reference not feeling valued, not being able to speak freely, or more simply put, having a lousy boss. In the past, it would have been considered radical to claim that most people would put having a good boss on par with making more money. Human resource executives often tell me that in exit interviews an employee may say he is leaving because the new job pays more. But when you ask him why he started looking in the first place, he replies that he started looking for another job because of a bad boss. So even when some people say they left because of better pay, the real truth is they never would have left if they had high-trust relationships with their bosses.

Let me underscore the relationship between retention and trust. Trust is clearly the central element to people feeling valued. Reduce trust and you eliminate the ability for a boss or organization to value their people. Increase trust and the bonds between employee and boss are remarkably resilient. Therefore, there is a major shift underway—organizations are being forced to embrace the idea of being a partner instead of a boss. While fear is the primary currency of a boss, trust is the primary currency of a partnership. From a supply and demand standpoint, trust's stock is going up. It may be in low supply in many organizations, but the need to compete in a global economy is fueling greatly increased demand.

Low trust increases turnover.

Because of the complexity of the workplace and the related cost of integrating a new person into a team today, turnover is a much more monitored problem or metric. Therefore, low trust that increases turnover can no longer be written off as a "personality conflict with the boss." If you want to compete and provide excellence that will create sustained growth and you are in a "first-world" (as opposed to third-world) country, you have to conclude that high-trust relationships between manager and employee reduce turnover, reduce cost, and ensure the retention of your best talent.

Don't get me wrong; this is an evolution not a revolution. You will still find plenty of low-trust managers and organizations for many years to come that will be profitable. But their profitability will last only as long as they don't feel global competition requiring them to add value and to become creative.

Talent Retention and Baby Boomer Retirement

With low unemployment, organizations are challenged to find and keep good talent. Let's put this in practical terms. Think about the three best people that work for you. Then think about the ramifications of having one or two of them give you their notice tomorrow that they are retiring or taking a position elsewhere. I don't mean to cause you anxiety, but the loss of talented people puts far more demand on you and adds a lot of challenge to your success. And as the United States heads into a season of baby boomers retiring, we are going to lose a lot of management talent. There are varying statistics on the "talent drain" as some call it. But all agree that it will put a higher premium on managers who can lead in such a way as to build loyalty and retention.

Arlene Dohm, an economist in the Office of Employment Projections for the Bureau of Labor Statistics, wrote the following as an introduction to her research paper titled, "Gauging the Labor Force Effects of Retiring Baby Boomers":

> As aging baby boomers begin retiring, the effects on the overall economy and certain occupation and industries will be substantial, creating a need for younger workers to fill the vacated jobs, many of which require relatively high levels of skill.

Ms. Dohm continues on to say that in the decade between 1988 and 1998, 19 million people left the workforce. But it gets worse. In the decade from 1998 to 2008, the number is predicted to rise to 25 million.

The reason this makes high trust so important, as I mentioned earlier, is that the people who will be replacing baby boomers are inherently less tolerant of bad working conditions and/or low trust bosses. Put another way, managers of all sectors consistently tell me that baby boomers tolerate bad bosses and bad working conditions far better than any other generation currently in the workforce. Indeed, younger generations are putting greater pressure on managers to operate with higher trust because they are far less likely to tolerate bad management.

One of the common explanations offered for this is that younger generations don't have the work ethic that baby boomers have. However, there is a different explanation in many cases. Younger generations are less tolerant of bad bosses and working conditions because they have more economic choice, so they appear to not want to work as hard. But in reality, they are challenging the boss and employer to do better. Some bosses construe this as a work ethic problem when it really is an economic issue and/or a trust issue.

Skilled Employees Require Skilled Leaders

Another employment shift is the growth in higher skilled jobs and therefore a need for higher skilled leadership. The industry that many feel has been hardest hit by the global economy with the loss of jobs is manufacturing. For example, while it is true that the United States has lost many low-skilled manufacturing jobs to outsourcing, the United States is also experiencing rapid growth in higher skilled jobs.

According to a study published in the Federal Reserve Bank of New York's February/March 2006 issue of *Current Issues in Economics and Finance,* high-skilled manufacturing jobs in the United States grew 37 percent between 1983 and 2002, while medium-skilled jobs decreased by 18 percent and low-skilled jobs by 25 percent. This means that even the sector hardest hit by global competition has to prepare managers to develop and retain these more highly skilled and thus more sought-after employees.

An interesting example of this is a story I heard on a recent trip to Pennsylvania about an owner of a manufacturing facility that creates plastic chemical tanks. The ability to find and develop higher skilled labor was cramping his company's ability to grow. He claimed that if he could have developed or found the higher skilled employees he needed, the output would have grown another 30 percent.

Managers need to cultivate talent to higher levels to be competitive and they must manage smarter to retain their talent because the pool of talent is highly sought after. Trust is integral to both developing and retaining people.

Cultural Case for Trust

People often ask me, "What is the most important thing a manager contributes to an organization?" There are many responses to that question, but one that stands out is the manager's ability to create an energized, innovative, and positive, high-trust culture. Table 2.1 shows the costs and benefits to a culture that result from a manager's ability or inability to build trust.

Table 2.1 Low–Trust versus High–Trust Business Cultures

Cost of Low Trust	*Benefit of High Trust*
A lack of clarity and hidden agendas cause project failure.	Strips away distractions and creates clarity to focus on the right things.
Higher stress and misdirected energy.	Lower stress and higher energy.
Reduced candor. Increased negative politics.	Increased candor with higher creativity and fewer negative conflicts.
Higher turnover.	Lower turnover because people feel valued.
Younger generations respond to low trust with a weaker work ethic and lack of patience.	All generations improve performance when trust is high. Trust is the one true bridge across all generations.

Table 2.1 *(Continued)*

Cost of Low Trust	Benefit of High Trust
Low trust translates into a caustic or cold place to work, which reduces the company's ability to retain and attract talent. Employees caution people to stay away.	High trust permits a more fulfilling workplace and generates warmth that retains and draws talent. Employees are far more likely to refer and recruit talent.
Employees reduce risk taking and stop innovating.	Employees are more empowered to take risks and innovate.
Employees are afraid to share knowledge because they perceive knowledge as power in a low-trust culture.	Employees share knowledge because they trust that their boss knows their true value.
Low trust fosters a focus on self-preservation and creates silos. The resulting selfishness prevents partnership and collaboration within silos and between them.	Partnerships and collaborations flourish because the primary catalyst for them (leadership by example) is intact. The walls that create silos have no foundations on which to stand.
Development occurs at a slower rate.	Development occurs at a rapid rate.
Universally, people dislike being surrounded by people they do not trust; work becomes drudgery.	Universally, people want to be surrounded by people they trust; work becomes a second home.

Summary

The importance of this book is heightened by global economics that are fueling fierce competition, which is forcing people and organizations to embrace the idea of partnership with their customers, employees, and even their vendors. While fear is the primary currency of a boss, trust is the primary currency of a leader.

3 | Four Competencies that Build Radical Trust

The leadership trust model in Figure 3.1 identifies the four competencies that great leaders develop to build Radical Trust. The good news is that most people have developed some level of competency with all of these. The problem with most of us is that we are often really good with one or a couple of these four competencies, but we have weaknesses in others that are costly.

For example, there are many managers who are great with Execution Trust, but can't go to the next level because of a lack of competency in Communication Trust or Loyalty Trust. This is common among entrepreneurial types who can drive results, but who also drive people crazy. The careers of these entrepreneurs are often stunted when growth or higher-level management responsibilities call for more in the way of what some call *people skills*.

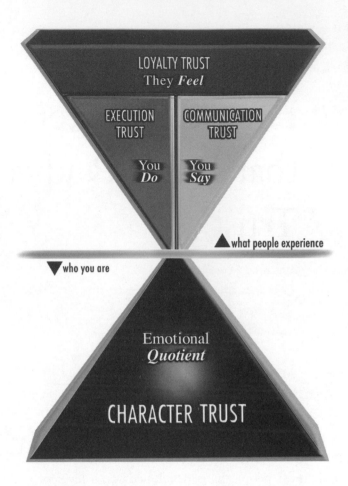

Figure 3.1 Healey Leadership Trust Model

Alternatively, there are many gifted communicators who have wide popularity in a culture, but who have not mastered Execution Trust and can't be relied on to deliver. There are also many who possess extremely valuable expertise, but do not succeed in management because they have yet to develop Execution or Communication Trust.

This is very common among healthcare, pharmaceutical, financial, and legal professionals who are well educated and talented, but who have deficiencies in these competencies. Their significant knowledge and skill is marginalized by these deficiencies. I have had the pleasure of watching some of these executives fulfill their potential and make many more contributions once they master the right competencies. Over the years, many have expressed the simple truth that they just didn't know how important these other aspects of leadership were.

These competencies are also critical for those who are in a *matrixed environment*. Matrix refers to people who have to get others to cooperate with their projects but don't have formal authority over those people. The less formal name for this skill is "begging." Success in this type of matrixed, or flat, organization requires one of the central outcomes of mastering these competencies: The ability to influence others to gain buy-in and cooperation.

In this book, I will show you how to raise the bar with each of these competencies and how to shore up any gaps that may exist. When managers more fully master these competencies, title and formal authority become much less important. The trust model in Figure 3.1 depicts the four competencies that are needed to be successful as a leader in today's world and how to exercise influence in your career and personal life.

The Four Competencies

Character Trust

Character Trust refers to the way we, as leaders, consistently enable our values to drive our execution and communication so others trust us enough to give loyalty. Leadership traits that are critical in business today such as transparency, directness, decisiveness, energy, perceptiveness, and many others require a depth of character.

Character development is sometimes referred to as *emotional quotient* (EQ). Because EQ or character impacts performance, organizations are beginning to recognize the benefit of making character or EQ growth a part of the development that occurs in the workplace.

You will see how today's great leaders rely on their strength of character as a powerful tool to influence change and the development of EQ in others. They take very seriously their own character and recognize that their character provides a foundation for all the other leadership competencies (as the model illustrates). It drives our ability to build trust because it colors the way we execute, communicate, and establish loyalty. It represents *who we are* at a core level. It is through the ongoing development of character, that Radical Trust leaders are able to win people's respect and cooperation.

In Part III, where we will cover the competency Character Trust, we take a practical approach to both developing your character and coaching others to develop their EQ. More and more organizations are emphasizing these *core values* as a way to focus and develop employees to exhibit character traits that lead to success.

When people experience a manager with strong character or high EQ, it is like being preapproved for a mortgage. The bank (employee, vendor, or customer in this case) is willing to execute on your behalf immediately and with speed because they have already verified you and your standing and have already made a commitment at a fundamental level to you (loyalty). This speeds everything up.

Execution Trust

Execution Trust relates to what you do and are able to get others to do. It relates to people trusting a manager's promise to deliver tasks and actions or goods and services on time. New managers often quickly identify this as a serious struggle because it is hard for them to learn to juggle competing demands. Mid-level and senior managers find execution to be particularly daunting during times of change.

If you can build Execution Trust, you create collaboration, which drives on-time delivery. When managers need to execute an organization's mission, there are two fundamental things they have to master: the strategic aspect and the people side. For many leaders, gaps often appear in this competency because they know what the right strategies and/or priorities are, but they fail to effectively engage people to execute.

Communication Trust

Communication Trust enables people to trust what we say and what they learn from us. An often-repeated mantra in organizations is that 90 percent of problems stem from communication. In Part IV, we will teach you some critical, but neglected, links between communication and character. It may surprise you how much easier it is to be an effective leader/communicator when you permit your character to steer your messages.

People are much more responsive to leaders who communicate in an authentic fashion. Talented people have little tolerance for the superficial, feelings-based communications techniques that flourished in the last half of the twentieth century. The material in Part IV frees you from many of the cumbersome communication practices that are unproductive. I reveal a simple set of traits that easily piggyback on the sound character and communication practices you have already established.

Even though some of the strategies I give you actually simplify the way you communicate, you will also create better and deeper understanding, buy-in, and responsiveness. This competency will help even seasoned senior leaders avoid communication blunders that minimize credibility.

Loyalty Trust

Loyalty Trust means that people believe that you will look out for them and their interests. This encourages people to take risks—to work hard toward shared goals faithfully because they believe you are behind them; you will back them up and you will stand by them.

In Part V, you will learn how Loyalty Trust stimulates a higher level of personal investment that fosters deeper levels of commitment and vulnerability. This permits you to influence people at deeper levels and creates faster decision making and greater cooperation. This is what makes strong partnerships valuable.

When healthy loyalties are intact, new ideas are implemented more quickly and conflict and stress are naturally handled in a more productive fashion. Loyalty Trust creates the type of bond or partnership that brings out the best in people and causes them to be compelled to perform at their best.

The methods and ideas presented, related to these competencies, make the building of trust an integral part of how you manage. So in an age when speed is essential, you will see that this book does not ask you to do things that take more time. You will find ideas that get you working smarter. In fact, you will be surprised at a few of the things these leaders say you should *stop* doing.

The natural result of integrating these competencies into the way you live is that you will have more loyalty. Loyalty is a powerful motivational force. The good news for you if you are a typically busy manager is that these ideas will allow you to build from your current capabilities with each of these competencies. You will appreciate the realism that is inherent to these strategies. This book shows you practical and effective ways to lead execution and to communicate as a leader so that you earn trust and its rich payoff: loyalty.

Figure 3.2 illustrates why leaders who build Radical Trust are so successful—they create a large platform for the success of a great many people.

Cost of Broken Trust

We live in an age where the cost of broken trust is being trumpeted in the media and where employee surveys are showing that there is an

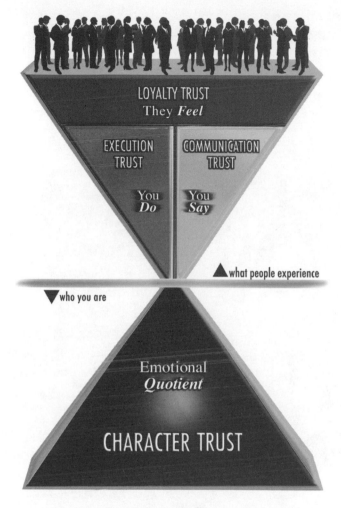

Figure 3.2   A Foundation for Success

inherent mistrust inside many organizations with employees and outside with customers or vendors. Figure 3.3 illustrates the consequences of this.

It is also important to note that often a lack of trust comes not from intentional wrongs, but because managers are out of touch with

Figure 3.3   The Cost of Broken Trust

the ramifications of what they say and do. I have seen many managers who never get comfortable being a leader. They feel like they are wearing someone else's skin or playing a role. People who don't feel and act naturally are far more likely to be out of touch with the consequences of what they say and do, and that almost always marginalizes relationships and lowers productivity in a workforce or customer/vendor relationship.

The consequences depicted in Figure 3.3 are the same regardless of whether our actions or words are intentional or unintentional. This book helps you grow and teach others to grow in each of these four competencies that build Radical Trust in ways that are practical and authentic.

A Note about How This Book Is Organized

In the business world how we execute is the primary competency on which leaders are judged, so it is practical to make Execution Trust the first of the four competencies of this model we explore in the next part of this book. Discussing Execution Trust first will also create a more practical framework for our discussions of Character Trust, Communication Trust, and Loyalty Trust that will follow.

PART II

Execution Trust
(What You Do)

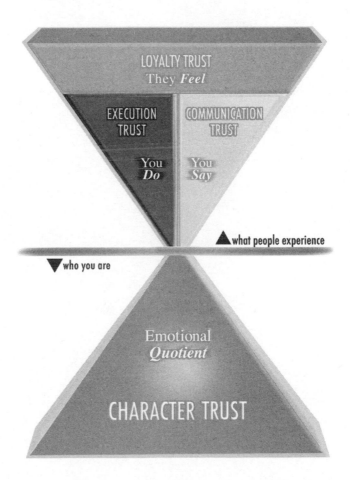

4

Be a Leader Who Can Execute

> *A great deal of a leader's value is determined by his or her ability to attract and grow talent. In a global economy, talent is the key to execution and revenue growth.*

Inherent in today's business climate is the need to execute well while implementing change to innovate and grow your business. Being good at leading execution while growing your team, business unit, or company requires, more than anything else, that you be good at engaging and unleashing talent. The leadership principles to build the kind of trust that permits a leader to engage talent are the same whether you are a manager, a senior executive, a sales and marketing manager, an operations manager, or any other type of leader. The stress of competition demands that every

37

leader in an organization be more effective at helping talent expand their capacity.

You may have noticed that I have been talking about engaging and unleashing talent, but I have not used the word *develop*. Before I use that word, I want to be careful to define what effective leaders do to help people be successful. The most productive contributions leaders make to a person's ability to execute have more to do with helping them find, release, and add skill to talent they already possess. This is a critical aspect of development that some call *coaching*.

The kind of coaching I am referencing requires leaders to build strong, high-trust relationships with their people to be able to exercise a catalytic influence. The stronger the trust or bond between the leader and his or her people, the better the development and the better the execution. I illustrate that with the following case study.

I took a cab from O'Hare Airport to the GAP's Chicago offices to meet Steve Krajenka and his management team. The cabby was pointing out the gleaming retail landmarks on the renowned Miracle Mile. As he dropped me off at the GAP office in the midst of this shopping extravaganza, it was clear that Steve's team was in a business that contended with fierce competition.

I stepped off the elevator and walked through the glass doors bearing GAP's logo. I was meeting with Steve's management team to strategize for a leadership development session we were having with all his managers the next afternoon. No one was in the waiting area. I could hear a group of people in a conference room not too far away. I remember thinking it sounded more like the banter and energy that you might hear and feel at a family gathering. The voices sounded bold but friendly, like strong-willed family members who had a healthy bond and were debating back and forth. As I turned the corner and came into sight, Steve jumped up and greeted me with a natural warmth that was indicative of what was to come.

This energetic and family-like atmosphere captures the essence of why Steve is so successful as a leader. I have chosen him to model Execution Trust because he knows how to rally talent to achieve results. In the past five years, the term *execution* has come to represent the ability to create and synchronize complex change and action that culminates in pleasing customers and making profits.

The use of this term in business stems from the traditional use of the word execution to describe a symphony playing a large-scale musical work like one of Beethoven's sonatas. Success in the complex world of business today requires the same kind of focus and orchestration to harness talent to produce something that is pleasing to others.

Oddly, the fact that the word also means to kill represents well the number of managers who, unlike Steve, achieve their execution excellence by driving people with fear and manipulation.

As the atmosphere in the conference room revealed, Steve is like an orchestra leader who treats his people like talented musicians rather than labor cost to be managed.

Steve has had a long history of success starting out as a buyer and department manager for JC Penney and working his way up to senior leadership positions with noteworthy retailers. He was the vice president of stores for the Limited, senior vice president for retail operations for Discovery Stores, and vice president of stores worldwide for Sunglass Hut International.

Steve took two years off to invest time at home with his wife Kathy and two teenage sons during what was an important time for his family. During that sabbatical from retail, he also filled a leadership role at his church. I recently got a call from Steve letting me know he had taken a position as director of stores for Martin + Osa. This is a new brand he will build for American Eagle Outfitters.

My work with Steve took place during his very successful career at the GAP where he was a district manager, director of stores for their Hemisphere premium brand, GAP regional director, regional vice president, and finally zone vice president for the Midwest. His results speak for themselves. As I mentioned earlier, within one year of Steve contributing his leadership to the Midwest Zone, they were number one in sales.

The GAP is well known for its execution excellence. When you walk into a GAP store, you find things are orderly, inventory is more plentiful, and the experience of getting in and out is efficient. Re-markably, GAP has merged this more rigorous side of business (execution) with a clothing brand that reaches the buyer's emotional side by providing intriguing style choices.

I use four different leaders in this book to illustrate these competencies because, although what I am going to reveal to you may seem easy, it clearly takes a unique kind of commitment. This is especially true related to this topic of execution, which is usually a topic that is considered rigorous and filled with high discipline, conformity, and sacrifice. You will be pleasantly surprised at the way Steve achieved success with far less stress and had fun while doing it because of the way he made trust central to achieving execution excellence.

5

Use Trust to Tap and Unleash Talent

The spirit of the Christmas season of 2005 spurred a former manager of Steve's, Lesli Gilbert, to send Steve a Tiffany's crystal apple with a note that said: "Best teacher I ever had." I want to introduce Lesli to you. She met Steve in 1995 when she managed a store for the Limited clothing retailer and Steve was her boss's boss.

Lesli followed Steve many times as his career advanced because she so valued his leadership. Over the 10 years of their relationship, Lesli went from being a store manager for the Limited to senior director of operations, adult brands, for the GAP.

Lesli is one of many extremely talented leaders whom Steve identified and developed with his mentoring style. Although we will cite other talented leaders Steve has mentored, Lesli and Steve's story is central proof of the power of Radical Trust to create execution excellence.

Steve rarely goes through the more common approach to leadership in which the leader starts out by giving minimal responsibility, doing close monitoring, then gradually giving the subordinate more freedom. Steve accelerates the contributions of his people and saves a ton of time by building the kind of trust that allows him to mentor instead of manage. This requires a leader to be willing to do a better job identifying talent. The leader must create a highly transparent relationship that reduces the risk of giving more trust early.

Engaging Talent

Leaders need a high level of trust to be able to supersede boundaries and turf to identify, develop, and promote talent.

There are many tools, such as assessments, that managers can use to increase their odds of identifying talent. And there is some great work that human resource professionals are doing to partner with managers to assist in identifying talent. I will show you later how Steve relies on a strong relationship with his human resources partner.

However, Steve insists that no one owns the right to develop people. So there is no chain-of-command issue that blocks trust and communication on his teams. His people love the way he creates partnerships that don't rely on formal titles and organization charts.

Interestingly, Steve's managers are delighted that Steve reaches past them directly to his subordinates to identify and develop talent. It goes the other way as well. All the associates in Steve's business units feel they can reach out to whatever leader they need to get the job done. He makes it clear that they all share in each other's success.

Just prior to Steve leaving the GAP to take a sabbatical, his team gave him a book inscribed with 50 testimonials from managers throughout the Midwest. Since Steve often referenced Jim Collins's book, *Good to Great*, his team bound expressions of thanks and titled it *Good to Great—Steve Krajenka*. Here is one of several excerpts I will share with you. This one supports my claim that Radical Trust leaders break down walls. They encourage all players to be eager to partner with whomever necessary to grow and execute at higher levels:

> I wanted to thank you . . . for being a great support to my career and my managers! Your efforts to move the Zone and Company forward will be missed. . . . I have been inspired after every conversation we have had. Thank you for spending time with my managers, whether it was during a visit or a meeting you always have respected their position and spoke to them like an equal. You have made such a difference in how I make business decisions and how my managers and I inspire our employees. Thank you Steve. . . .
>
> —Laura Klejka, GAP District Manager

Simple Ways to Identify Talent and Future Partners

Here are three steps that Steve believes have allowed him over a long and successful career to accurately identify talent. He has found that these steps have enabled him to have a 90 percent accuracy rate in getting the talent he needs to execute:

1. He requires proof that they have done something in a previous role that was recognized by someone else as going above and beyond. "Being promoted is a sign of this. Or they initiated something that was adapted or bought into by someone else." During an interview, he asks questions of candidates that let them share how they have provided contributions that went

beyond the typical responsibilities. But he is sure to validate this with references from third parties.

2. He looks for a balanced life. "People who can speak as passionately about their personal life as their professional life let me know that they are responsible. If all their success and satisfaction hangs on their career, it puts undue pressure on us as a company to be responsible to make them happy."

3. Strong communication skills—specifically, candor and transparency. "I try to find out if they hold back on what they feel and think. If they are open with me in the interview, then I can count on them to tell me what they think and what is going on. If they are reluctant to be open in the interview, then I don't want to work with them. People who bottle things up inside have a hard time creating excellence. It is harder for them to take feedback and grow."

Lesli says, "His questions are genuine attempts to allow employees to identify their strengths and weaknesses, so Steve can engage their talent. But he is relentless about peeling back the layers of the onion. And he does not apologize for it."

6

Solid Relationships Drive Solid Execution

> *Execution trust begins with making a commitment to someone else's success.*

Steve met Lesli while he was visiting Limited stores. She was a store manager. "When I met Lesli working in one of our stores, I knew I met someone special that I could invest in. And I told her that." Steve saw Lesli's talent, drive, and maturity and engaged her at a high level immediately.

This is a key trait related to trust. Steve, like many great leaders, is quick to embrace talent. He does not do a lot of pondering and he does not solely rely on formal testing or evaluations. He looks at recent results, in-person interaction, and relies on other trusted leaders who say, "This person is a talent."

As soon as Steve has enough evidence that this person is a talent, he begins to extend trust. Steve does this by candidly expressing the truth in what he sees. It is very motivating when you hear a leader proclaim faith in you. Lesli was clearly motivated the day Steve told her what he saw in her. As soon as he finishes building the person up by expressing what he sees, Steve is very candid about asking the person to commit to a higher level of development and effort. Steve says, "What I make sure I do at the beginning of the relationship is let the person know we have an attachment."

Steve's decision to engage with Lesli and create an attachment paid off in the form of bottom-line results very quickly. She went from store manager to district manager and turned around a very sluggish district.

In the big picture, Lesli made a major contribution to Steve's over-all bottom line at the Limited. They achieved the first sales increase in five years. This represented an incremental volume increase of 10.5 percent, and they reduced operating expenses by $3 million.

It is important to note that at that time (in the mid-1990s), the Limited was a post-peak company. It sometimes is easier to build trust and to lead when an organization is growing and there is excitement and financial opportunity cultivated by that growth. Conversely, when an organization is flat or on a down-slope financially, it is usually much more challenging to build trust. But Steve and Lesli proved that Radical Trust can be achieved in spite of the circumstances around you.

What Steve did here was critical to his and his team's success. We often have a choice as to whether we micromanage people or empower them with a more interdependent mentoring relationship that allows them to have more freedom. This allows the manager to have more time for other matters.

Using Trust to Reduce Costly Micromanagement

> *Relationship-management is more productive than micromanagement.*

So in the example with Lesli, Steve made a choice as to how he managed. This brings up a critical management question: Should you focus your time on helping your most talented managers grow to new heights of performance as Steve did with Lesli? Or, should you focus your time on all the problem people who may meet failure if you don't ensure their success with a lot of micromanaging? This has become a big question in recent years. But I think we are asking the wrong question.

This question assumes the decision hinges on the talent and maturity of your employees. While that is relevant, I think the bigger question is: What is your management paradigm? Steve resists spending time micromanaging—that is his management paradigm. As you will see, as much as he cares about his people, he is very willing to let people go if it will help them move to a place where they don't have to be micromanaged.

> *People often micromanage because they lack the ability to build trust.*

For Steve to be successful in a management paradigm that requires giving a great deal of responsibility and freedom to talented people, he has to be great at building trust. I would argue that the real question for you is not whether you tend to micromanage or mentor, but whether you are good at building trust. If you are not competent in all the competencies for building trust, you are forced to do more micromanaging—even of talented people who don't need it.

The good news is that while Radical Trust employee-manager relationships are rare, they are not hard to create with talented people. Here are the five steps Steve takes with every person who has accountability to him:

Five Steps to Getting the Best from Talented People

1. Express and confirm the talent you see.
2. Tell them the expectation you have.
3. Make it clear that it is their responsibility to achieve results.
4. Make it clear that your contribution is to help remove roadblocks and solve problems they cannot solve.
5. Give them permission to contact you for help. Make this clear so they truly feel your availability and set parameters so it is productive for you. You don't just want to be accessible. You want to be welcoming. You need to ensure that they see this as a relationship. That is the secret. The relationship places positive tension on them to exceed your expectations.

As soon as Steve sees talent, whether it is in an interview or when meeting internal talent, he lets them know they can go places and challenges them to put in the effort by following these five steps.

He has found that, for many people, this is the first time a manager has really been serious about investing in their success. "People get excited and inspired with this idea that there is a serious attachment between us and that it is focused on mutual success."

Lesli accepted Steve's challenge and began to see herself as a partner instead of as an employee. She eagerly accepted more responsibility and made bigger and bigger contributions at the Limited.

Talent Naturally Follows Leaders

Lesli valued Steve's ability to develop her and create opportunities so much that she staked her career on it and followed Steve from the

Limited to the GAP, to the Discovery Stores, and back to the GAP where, today, she is a senior executive at GAP headquarters in San Francisco.

When Steve left the GAP and went to the Discovery Company to pioneer the opening of their retail stores, he called Lesli and made her an offer. In Lesli's words, "Steve called and said I want you to come down here and take a position for me that will amount to a demotion." What made his request harder is that she would have to move her family from New Jersey to Atlanta. Steve was a trusted leader, but was she willing to stake her career on him and make this kind of a move that would uproot her family, especially one that involved a demotion?

Lesli went home and said to her husband, Bob Gilbert, "Steve made me a job offer. . . . It will not be a promotion. . . . It will require a move to Atlanta." As she heard herself describe the opportunity out loud, Lesli said, "I felt worse about it and had doubts."

"The more I thought about it, the only thing attracting me to it was my trust in Steve." Her husband immediately said, "Let's do it." He knew the strength of Lesli's and Steve's working relationship and knew it assured Lesli a successful future. He also knew how rare it was to have that level of trust in the workplace. However, Lesli confessed, "It took me 10 days of vacillating back and forth before I decided to do it." As you will see, this and other decisions to trust Steve ultimately led Lesli to a career path of success.

Let's examine what Steve does that would inspire an associate to change jobs multiple times and take career risks just to be part of his team.

7 | How Leaders Marry Time and People

Many people make the mistake of thinking that disciplined time management practices are the key to execution excellence. When I asked Steve about how he finds the time to provide all the coaching he practices, he said, "I can't afford *not to coach*." When I further pressed him for any time management tips that he uses to assure that he is in tune with his people and able to be fully engaged, he again said, "It is not about time management."

He went on to explain that by making coaching a part of his normal interaction, he saves countless hours that others lose because he is proactive. Another way of saying this is that most managers try to squeeze coaching in last and often fail to do it effectively. As a result, they put themselves and their employees in a reactive and time-wasting cycle. So it is no surprise that managers who aren't in tune with their people feel starved for time.

I think Steve's response is consistent with many other effective leaders. Most managers have the question reversed. The question is not: How do you manage your time to allow you to be effective with feedback? The question is: How can you get anything done if you don't provide immediate and ongoing feedback to your people? Steve believes the consequence of delayed feedback is a lot of wasted time later.

Steve says that he tells people, "Don't make me work to uncover the truth." Less functional managers waste huge amounts of time because of a failure to achieve transparency.

Set an Expectation for Full Disclosure

> *A leader's criticism doesn't compromise a relationship. It deepens it.*

When I asked Steve about how he sets an expectation for transparency, he said with passion, "Trust is about full exposure. Be open about what you personally are working on in your own development. I try to create a natural sort of 360-degree environment." Referring to the practice of getting feedback about your performance from *all* the people you impact—360-degree means bosses, peers, subordinates, and in some organizations, even customers and vendors. Organizations rightly spend a lot of money administering tools and processes to achieve a high level of candor and feedback. Steve makes it a part of how he communicates.

Most 360-degree feedback causes people to *be* candid instead of teaching them *how* to be candid. In other words, most instruments that are used today for what we call 360-degree feedback are giving people fish, not teaching them how to fish. I have created a process through my training and consulting practice that focuses on teaching leaders to do what Steve does so that the relationship becomes the on-going vehicle. The instrument is only the catalyst.

In fact, society in general is so dysfunctional that often candid feedback on 360-degree evaluations is anonymous to permit people to be more honest and to minimize retribution.

And the traditional annual or even quarterly reviews provide only minimal talent development and are often used as the vehicle for justifying disciplining people and giving raises. But they cannot replace the habitual practice of candid, frequent feedback like Steve trains his managers to provide.

The subject of developing talent is incomplete if we don't talk about the reality of firing people that is part of life at most organizations. If done correctly, firing is an integral part of development. But it will be more productive to discuss this topic after we have introduced the ideas on Communication Trust. And because firing is central to loyalty, I cover it in the last competency—Loyalty Trust.

Give Timely Feedback

Steve likens the constant willingness to give feedback, be it praise or criticism, to creating a sense of belonging. He says, "If you want to create a sense of belonging, you make feedback natural— in the moment. If I wait three months, it may become defensive and it has lost context." You will see more about this in our part on Communication Trust where we link setting context to the ability to convey effective messages. Setting context is what a leader does to keep talented people's energy focused on the right things.

> *Candid and frequent feedback focuses talented people on the right actions that produce the right results.*

Feedback between leader and employee needs to occur more often than quarterly or yearly. One of the reasons annual or quarterly reviews are so dreaded and waste so much time is that they are missing the immediacy and clarity of being in the moment. Trying to re-create all those moments and squeeze them into an hour review session can take a lot of time and in the end provide only moderate feedback, little urgency, and a minimized chance for real change.

> *Great leaders don't count on annual or quarterly formal evaluations as their primary vehicle to develop talent.*

Use quarterly or annual evaluations as a tool to document raises and legal requirements. But plan on personal, regular, and immediate feedback as your primary vehicle for talent development.

Here is what Lesli had to say about this, "Back when I first met Steve and was a store manager, I had a broken team. There was a lack of trust in regional managers because there was such high turnover that there was no frequency of feedback. We were also missing the key piece: trust. We did not have managers who were direct with feedback and open enough to tell you the good, bad, and ugly."

Steve said, "I also don't believe it is effective to set 'touch-base' time. For example, I used to set aside a certain time I was available to my managers, say from 1 to 2 on a particular day. And they could call me and know I was accessible." He felt this could lead to wasted time because subordinates feel compelled to call even if they don't need to touch base. He finds it better to just give them his cell phone number and be available to them.

Steve wants to empower them to drive the agenda and use him as a problem solver and roadblock remover. It is important to add that even though Steve's people know they can contact him any time, they respect his time and only call when they need him. And because the relationship is so transparent and expectations are clear, many of his conversations with his people mirror the productive and quick conversations we have with close friends.

I have noticed that when Steve finishes a conversation with a manager, he is off the phone in a heartbeat. As soon as the need has been addressed, he says, "See ya! Bye." It sounds like he is talking with an old friend who needs no pretense or drawn-out interaction.

Save Time by Letting Your People Set Agendas

Another thing Steve does that saves a ton of time and achieves a high level of understanding is that he asks his people to set and drive the agenda for most conversations. This assures that they get what they need, and usually gives him what he needs. They then feel he is very accessible, and it makes his job easier.

Here are some rules Steve follows to further maximize his busy schedule:

Three Ideas to Make Time Work for You

1. Delegate to those who have earned it.
2. Hire talent and don't micromanage employees.
3. With each seasoned person you manage, pick at least one complex area you suspect he or she may struggle with. Then, drill to a deep level of detail on it, so you "fly high" with most things except this one item. Steve refers to this as "Fly high and dig deep." He feels it keeps people on their toes. There is an incredible sense of entitlement to all of that because people know you trust them to give them space. But they know you are also engaging to check up. Steve cautions,

"Don't fly too high and be a generalist. And don't dig deep on everything so you micromanage."

> **The ability to drill down and uncover root causes opens the door to great solutions.**

A Few More Thoughts on Time, Execution, and Trust

Steve feels many managers waste time because they are too willing to share in people's workloads. Many managers incorrectly think they have to build trust with people by pitching in and helping them with their responsibilities. Steve makes it clear that he "doesn't play in their sandbox."

His people hold no resentment. Consider this feedback from one of Steve's managers:

> You have been such an inspiration to the Zone, from regional managers to heads of stores to the sales associates. In a world of fast-paced business, it was very nice for my Zone vice president to always take time out for me!
>
> —Vicki Hospodka, Regional Executive Assistant

Steve also believes that pressuring people to take responsibility creates great passion and that creates a significant time management gain. "When you build responsibility and passion around a company, everyone operates at a higher level because they share a common set of goals or even dreams."

Another thing Steve does that helps him is to write everything down in a journal. "That process puts it in my memory and my people know I write it down."

8

How to Sustain Drive in a Culture

We just laid out a practical foundation for how a Radical Trust leader creates execution excellence. A specific case-study with Steve and Lesli demonstrated the direct connection between trust, execution, and bottom-line success. This provided practical insights into how to identify and engage talent, how relationships create a culture that strives for excellence, how you preserve time so you can build trust and how to move away from time-consuming and performance-draining micromanagement. Now let's move through a series of ideas and practices that will sustain the kind of trust that maintains high levels of drive and performance.

How to Make Feedback Positive and Solution Focused

> *We have nothing to fear, but fear itself.*
> *—Franklin D. Roosevelt*

Trust is often diminished and execution slowed because people are threatened by feedback. Feedback is far less frightening than the consequences of a lack of feedback. Lesli agrees, "Because Steve is so bold about giving feedback, he is perceived as very real and authentic." Most managers are too worried about the right time to give feedback. With Steve, it is an ongoing part of the relationship. If he sees something worthy of comment, he immediately engages.

But according to Lesli, one thing that makes interaction flow so smoothly is that, "He asks for input and he asks where opportunity is. He wants to be in your place to understand how you came to a decision. He asks the right questions to get to root causes."

Using Questions to Drive Results

Lesli said Steve usually funnels problems through lots of questions. The first time she met Steve he said, "Tell me about what has made you successful; how did you get where you are?"

Lesli describes this style of constantly being in problem-solving mode as, "His method is to start with putting you at ease at the beginning and then to build understanding from there."

> *You can always be fair, you can always be real, you can always be honest and still be very inspiring.*
> —*Steve Krajenka*

Early in their relationship, before Steve knew Lesli well, she sat down and had a conversation with him about wanting an opportunity to move up to a district manager position. She was in the middle of six people on the list to be considered. He probed hard about what she saw as her strengths and weaknesses. He felt she honestly assessed her situation as being capable in some areas but still inexperienced in others.

Steve ultimately was unclear about who was the best candidate and wasted no time about expressing how he saw it to Lesli. So she was clear that he had doubts.

Later Steve told her, "We are going to make you acting district manager. You show me what you can do." She would be acting district manager for a probationary period. Even though he saw talent, when Steve felt something was a stretch, he was frank about it.

Lesli said, "I felt Steve was taking a chance on me. I knew everything I did was a reflection of his trust in me so I wanted to make him proud." After many years, she still remembers her first in-depth conversation with Steve after taking over as acting district manager. It was classic Steve, "What do you like? What do the numbers look like? How is it supervising former peers? What is the biggest obstacle and how are you handling it? How do you treat people fundamentally?"

Another aspect of problem solving with Steve is he purposefully maintains a high level of energy that is contagious. It is as if he is fully aware that there is an opportunity right then and there for great stuff to happen and he is going to help push any breakthrough he can.

Responding to Bad News and Problems

After Lesli moved to Atlanta to work with Steve, she was a district manager and, in her words, "things were a mess in the district" when she got there. Within a short time after her arrival, Steve went on store visits with her.

"We walked into one mall and the store manager was sitting in front of her store because she had forgotten her keys." They had come to this store to participate in interviewing some new employees. Lesli said, "I turned to Steve and said have you ever done interviews in

front of a store before?" He said, "There is a first time for everything." After the interviews, Steve and I went to the car and I put my
head on the steering wheel and said, "Tell me if I still have a job."
Lesli fondly remembers Steve's response, "Lesli stop. Don't stress out.
Let's go to the next store." Steve understood that Lesli had only been
there a short time and was not responsible for this district's problems.
But he respected her because now that she was there, she wanted to
own both the good and bad. Steve said to her, "This is great! The way
you handled this confirms for me what kind of leader you are. You
care and you own it."

Lesli said, "That was a defining moment. The way he handled
that taught me a lot about grace under fire. It's not about what hap-
pens, it's the way you handle it."

"In all the years I worked for him, I never saw him raise his voice or
yell at someone. It is his consistency that makes me want to work with
him." And because of their relationship, all she needed in terms of frequency even with this troubled district was to talk every couple weeks.

Steve feels strongly that if employees know they can talk to you
without negative emotional recourse, people share openly and waste
a lot less time.

The Power of Being Consistent

One of the biggest differences between weak managers and high-
trust leaders is how they let the compression of time and events affect
how they carry themselves.

> *Leaders who navigate through the trials of their days, with a
> consistent demeanor are able to preserve the ability to observe,
> the discretion to engage, and a state of mind that can deal
> effectively in any situation.*

One reason managers refrain from giving timely feedback is that they permit themselves to be in a stressed, tired, preoccupied, or poor frame of mind that appears to negate their abilities. This is not an easy behavior to change. But it is worth changing. This, more than most behaviors, will prevent you from being promoted to a manager and will improve your own job satisfaction.

If you struggle with not having the energy to respond to people consistently, I recommend the book *The Power of Full Engagement* by Jim Loehr and Tony Schwartz (New York: Free Press, 2004). This book addresses the concept of managing energy instead of just managing time. The principles are very insightful about how you can maintain consistent energy.

The second thing to consider is that it is better to fumble through feedback than it is to delay it in most cases. As you force yourself to engage more often in spite of how you feel, you will be surprised how easy it is to switch into a feedback mode with your people regardless of what else is going on. And remember, by being timely with feedback, you are raising the level of urgency in the minds of your people.

Steve says, "Consistency is critical to trust. Being predictable is important to my people. Knowing that your boss will respond and react in the way you expect is a really good thing."

> *React to big things but don't react big to small things.*
> —*Steve Krajenka*

Criticism Should Elevate, Not Blame

Steve said, "I have found that many managers get trapped in the unproductive blame game because the emotion of the moment prevents them from organizing their thoughts." I have found that an easy-to-remember approach to avoiding blame and setting up constructive feedback includes the following steps represented by the acronym—FACE:

1. **F**rame the context of what you say by identifying the consequence or cost of the problem first. This underscores the importance of the discussion.
2. **A**sk them what happened and what can be done to improve or change the outcome the next time so that you become a coach instead of a lecturer.
3. **C**ommitment from them is the next step. Be sure to have their commitment to resolution. You want to be specific with complex issues and tie it to a date and/or metric.
4. **E**nd on a positive note. Give praise, if deserved, so that your feedback is balanced. Or end by focusing on the future.

There is a term that is very helpful to remember when giving critical feedback. That term is *solution orientation*. This means your orientation is strongly focused on solving problems and producing results.

9 | Getting People to Trust Metrics

Employees should see metrics as an ally in clarifying where to put focus. Because so many managers use metrics as a weapon to justify punishment, people tend to be intimidated by them. Worse yet, some managers think that simply barking at subordinates about their metrics is coaching. As a result, there is a lot of mistrust in metrics because of poor leadership.

A coaching client who is a vice president, Frank (name changed) manages several teams. He has committed to use metrics more effectively. To do that, he agreed to ensure his people got accurate metrics weekly so they could be more proactive. Metrics had been previously looked at only sporadically and were used as proof that action should be taken on a big problem. Therefore, at Frank's company, metrics were synonymous with crisis.

The first week Frank started this new dissemination of metrics, one of his key people saw metrics that made his team's work look weak. That manager approached Frank in an agitated state and began to justify the poor metrics. Frank responded with a supportive but candid tone and said, "You don't have to give me any justification. If you think these numbers are trending to a problem, do something about it. If you need help dealing with it just let me know."

The employee froze as if Frank had been speaking gibberish. It literally took him a couple of seconds to compute this new paradigm that Frank was expressing. The guy smiled, relaxed, and said, "Thanks, I'll let you know if I need you."

Metrics tell a story. Managers find ways to correct the story through feedback and problem solving. Frank commented later that his relationship with his people improved. More specifically, he said that there seems to be more trust and, as a result, more openness to talk about problems. The consistent use of accurate metrics that focus on what they already agreed was important, making it easier for everyone to communicate and deal with complex situations.

Seven Ways to Harness Metrics

1. They must be accurate at measuring specific outcomes.
2. They must be given frequently enough that they can be used proactively (most likely weekly or bimonthly). In some businesses, it is done daily.
3. Goals and expectations with metrics must be clear.
4. Any time there is change, you need to reconsider what and how you measure. Using metrics that were designed for an old business model is inaccurate and reduces trust.
5. Don't assume people understand what metrics are telling them. This is especially true with new talent and new metrics.
6. Measure only those things that are important to measure, otherwise you dilute the effectiveness of the good metrics from which you can run your business.
7. Never let metrics replace the relationship (the face or phone time communicating about complex business issues). Everything can't be distilled down to numbers.

> *Opportunities often lurk outside of what you track.*

When I asked Steve about how metrics come into play for him, he gave a response that I have heard him give before when he thinks something is fundamental to success. He said, "I can never *not* use metrics to help people in this business." He made an important point: He tries as much as possible to make his people part of the decision process to set metric goals. He said, "If I need a payroll percentage, let's agree on what that number is. If I have pressure to change something and I just tell you a new number, I am micromanaging you. I would rather treat you like a business person running a business and bring you into the decision."

Steve also expressed that there are plenty of tried-and-true metrics in their business model. "So unless you have an innovation that is radical, we are not going to waste time and open those metrics up for debate."

Further, Steve said he is big on "less is more" as a concept related to metrics. You can bury people in data if you are not careful.

Steve almost always uses metrics to facilitate discussion when he visits with his people. But metrics do not dominate. And most importantly, he says, "Seeing is important. It is very important that I don't overly rely on numbers. I need to get out and see what is going on with my eyes and ears."

Establishing Trust Stimulates Best-Practice Sharing

It is a wise and standard business practice to identify talented people who have excelled at something and have them teach others their best practices that earned them the great metrics. Then their metric becomes the new benchmark people are shooting for.

The problem with best practices is the devil is in the details. Since people readily see knowledge as power, it requires a lot of trust to ensure people share the true secrets that drive good numbers.

Further, some people just are not good at identifying or teaching others how they achieved success. So Steve recognizes that he and his managers need to pay attention to how systems and processes are used and modified for success.

> *Some managers mistakenly view metrics as the reality instead of a representation of a part of reality.*

Steve said, "You have to be careful that you don't over focus on the metrics. Be involved in systems and processes, not just results. The dialogue needs to be about what affected the results." He further modeled how he might say it, "Congratulations on the 24 percent increase. Tell me how you got there?" Steve gets very involved in setting up new systems and processes.

He agrees with an emerging school of thought about senior executives. Senior managers must be able to be trusted to have insight about how the business functions so they can marry their wisdom and experience to improving key systems and processes. In the old days, senior managers were excused from those details with the rationale that they were visionaries and had too many management things to do.

Steve is very careful to say that senior executives should not necessarily design and oversee all systems and processes. He tends to be involved with anything that involves changing metrics and key systems and processes. Steve is particularly careful to spend more time on metrics, systems, and processes with new managers during change or when results are scattered.

10 | Motivation: Beyond Wasteful Rewards and Negative Consequences

Steve thinks too much time and energy are wasted on rewards and consequences. Steve's people trust that if they perform at high levels, he will grow their careers. The fact that his people trust that eliminates the need for a lot of other rewards and consequences.

Further, Steve says, "The ability to execute is related to their own sense of excellence, so I don't have to attach rewards to things. For me and most of my people, 'the job well done' is the key."

Steve says that "the first person to know a job is well done is the individual." So the trust by the boss to let him or her experiment is part of the reward. Steve finds that he just doesn't have to spend a lot of time on rewards or consequences. Consequences can be as simple as: "I am disappointed or I expected more. I thought you said it would be done earlier." Because he has such high-trust relationships with his people, they truly are harder on themselves than any consequence he could level. So all he has to do is be prompt in his honesty.

His employees agree:

> I looked forward to your visits in my market, and I will miss having the opportunity to learn from you. Your passion for the employee journey and the external customer is contagious, and I appreciate your consistency in recognizing accomplishments. I have enjoyed your leadership.
>
> —Nicole Stivison, District Manager

Steve thinks that many managers make their jobs harder. They have a false expectation that a lot of praise or nasty consequences have to be doled out to get things done. It is easier and smarter to be simple and foster intrinsic motivation.

In this age of team building and stress on the importance of praise, it may also surprise you to hear Steve say, "I don't compliment the manager when the job meets the expectation." He does say thanks, "Thanks for being on time. . . . I appreciate that." However, he reserves praise for superior performance. He thinks a lot of managers use empty words. "If you can't attach a specific higher performance level to it, it's not a great job."

In summary, Steve says, "Set clear operating standards. Systematize mundane stuff so you and your people can get past that stuff to where they can have fun by making an impact. To do that, you have to be firm about what is not open to conversation and then people know where to focus their creative energy. If you help make them more efficient, people love you."

Harnessing the Best and Cheapest Motivator—Relationships

If you think any of what we have said in this chapter is contrary to a lot of the current teaching about motivation, you will crack-up at this one. Steve said, "I hate that fake team-building stuff. I don't have to make them feel warm or good. The relationship does!"

What I just shared with you may appear controversial or even contrary to modern team building. But the facts speak for themselves, and I am not talking about Steve's Zone's status as the number one Zone for GAP. I am speaking of his people's love of the way he leads. In a farewell letter to Steve, Sandy, a district manager said, "You are very consistent, emotionally mature, and you made it clear that we need to work to a high standard every day."

Steve says, "I don't tolerate talking to talk. . . . I don't want to know that you are just doing the job. Tell me what you are struggling with or things you can't control or new ideas. This saves us a lot of time."

Steve says, "Every day should be a good day." And he really believes it. He feels passionate that if he can help his people to have good days because they are so good at what they do, he doesn't need to spend all the extra time and company resources on rewards and consequences.

I want to cap off this chapter with a qualifying comment. Steve has the kind of work where he can build strong relationships with his people that are very rewarding. You may be in a setting where the relationships are not as strong or where employees are not as invested in their work.

If that is the case, you may need to do more praising and doling out of consequences than Steve would. But don't be too quick to think that praise, rewards, and consequences replace relationships. At the heart of this message is the power of relationships to hold people accountable and to motivate them.

I have seen other great leaders build similar kinds of inspiring relationships in spite of the fact that they may be the only leader doing so in that organization.

A couple of years ago, I was speaking about this very issue at a corporate leadership development session. During a break, a manager approached me and expressed how much she agreed. She was a very seasoned manager who was in her forties. She was one step away from the C-suite. Her boss was the CEO. Her eyes teared up when she explained that several years ago she had turned into the kind of boss she hated. In fact, she said she mirrored the bosses all around her.

After years of being treated like a robot by her boss and seeing other managers conduct themselves coldly, she said, "I just gave in to it." She went on to say, "There really is no meaningful excuse for me to treat people coldly just because that is the common practice in this culture."

She added, "I think I have become so focused on metrics that it has been a while since I mentored anyone. I used to think it was because we haven't been hiring talent. But I just realized that because I no longer engage with my people in a meaningful and transparent fashion, I really don't have a good read on what talent would be productive to mentor." And then she paused, and said with conviction, "I treat my people like my bosses treat me. And that is a damn poor excuse!"

Working in a cold culture with cold leaders is no excuse for you to lead poorly. Generate some heat!

11

Use Trust to Fuel Passion and Create Focus

There is a lot said today about the value of people having fun and having passion for what they do. It is clear that fun and passion are directly linked to execution excellence. Show me a leader who has Radical Trust, and I will show you employees who have more fun and passion.

Conversely, show me a manager who has low trust and you know that there are employees whose fun and passion are diminished. In fact, there is a lot of motivational hype that teaches superficial techniques for trying to create a fun- or passion-filled atmosphere. They all have to do with trying to raise the energy level with external motivators.

71

How Leaders Make Work Fun

It's not often that you are inspired and motivated by a visit from your Zone VP, but you gave my entire team from me to my managers right down to the last stock associate the energy for the upcoming weeks. Personally, you will be sorely missed. Thank you for giving me the opportunities to stretch myself and my capabilities. I get excited about my career and my team when I know someone can hear our voice and you were definitely that person. It's strange to think that in my 15-year retail career that I have never written a note to my executive team leaders until you, but your leadership was inspiring. I never left a meeting where you presented that I did not feel your energy or your passion for the people and the business.
                                    —Jodi Harker, District Manager

You may recall that Steve was candid with Lesli about asking her to prove herself and made her acting district manager. Lesli shares another example of how Steve builds trust and passion:

Four or five months after making me acting district manager, Steve met me at one of my stores with the human resources director. I was getting anxious because I felt I had proven myself and was looking for Steve to confirm my success. We went on to visit several stores. Steve seemed to be impressed. And he even said, "You own these stores!" But I was frustrated because he didn't yet appear willing to trust me and make me district manager. I said to myself that this was getting absurd. So I said to Steve, "What is going on?" He then went to his suitcase and surprised me by pulling out my new business cards that showed my title as District Manager. As he handed me the cards, he said, "I want you to call me any time."

I got mushy and teary-eyed. But I felt so validated to be trusted by a manager like Steve. Steve then said, "You have to go home and celebrate. You only get promoted to DM once in your life. Go celebrate with your family." I still tell my new DMs the same thing when I promote them.

Lesli and Steve's partnership remains strong to this day. In 2006, she was promoted to senior director of store operations, GAP brand. Her contribution has significantly expanded over time to now include a leadership role that impacts 25,000 associates and annual sales of $2.8 billion.

Leaders Need to Be Students

> *Most people guard what they say far too closely and therefore reserve vulnerability for a select few so to avoid risk. Radical Trust leaders are far less guarded and share themselves much more openly.*

The ability of a leader to learn and help create a culture of learners requires vulnerability to be modeled by the leader. Steve believes that to have on-going execution excellence, "everyone on the team has to be willing to be a learner. I want to work with people who are an open book—real people striving for excellence."

The problem is that in many organizations, managers don't model being a good student. Many managers mistakenly mask their deficiencies, and therefore, subordinates do the same. They hide their need for development.

Kay Prendergast was the human resources director for the GAP's Midwest Zone and worked closely with Steve. She is currently the director of human resources for Barnes & Noble and is an expert in human development. She was an eyewitness to Steve's leadership. Kay made an important observation about how vulnerability inspired Steve's culture to excellence:

He was very vulnerable. . . . From the beginning I could tell he was so open and confident. I remember him putting people at ease when he would say: "Oh my, I have no idea what that is." When you show that vulnerability, you impact the culture. People feel, "He's just like me! And I can share with him."

Kay went on to say, "I could always rely on him for candor, and he is always very truthful, direct, and authentic. In fact, he is always there. He will be there with whatever type of support he can provide. Steve is one of the best leaders I've ever worked with."

Here is a noteworthy aspect of how the GAP does business. They are unique in that their human resource professionals are serious business partners to line managers. During my work with Steve, I was inspired by how Steve and Kay worked on strategic goals together. She was very synchronized with his Zone's business goals; so much so that at the end of an in-depth meeting, I was very impressed to find out that Kay was not, as I thought, another Zone or regional manager.

Trust Is the Fertilizer of Passion

> *Steve has a contagious bias for action that infects others.*

There is a wonderful book I came across, *Making a Life, Making a Living,* by Mark Albion (New York: Warner Business Books, 2000). One of the leaders he profiled was Judy Wicks, the founder of an acclaimed restaurant in Philadelphia, the White Dog Café. It is known for its excellence in both service and food. I interviewed Judy for another book I was writing and, like Steve, I was struck by the way she was able to inspire a group of people who worked in a competitive and challenging sector.

The next time I was in Philadelphia, I sampled the White Dog Café and interviewed several employees. It totally validated what I had read. But what is interesting is what happened a year or so later.

I was speaking in Philadelphia at a conference on leadership and creativity. During a break, a gentleman approached me and said, "I can't tell you how much I agree with what you are saying about trust." As he said this, he handed me his business card and I noted it said, "Harry Kratz, General Manager, White Dog Café."

I was impressed that a guy who was general manager of a restaurant that had mastered leadership and creativity was attending a conference to learn yet more. He, like Steve, is always learning and that is contagious. When I asked Harry to summarize why the restaurant was successful at sustaining excellence, he said, "We have learned to foster people—not, drive them."

The following is an appropriate way to sum up Steve and this chapter on creating Execution Trust. It is another excerpt from the parting gift his managers at the GAP's Midwest Zone gave him when he left for his two-year sabbatical with his family:

> Steve, thank you for providing me the opportunity to "let my light shine." You are a leader who liberates, motivates, and elevates.
>
> —Anita Jenkins, Regional Manager

The cover of the book the employees called *Good to Great—Steve Krajenka* had the following inscription:

> Dedicated to
>
> Steven Krajenka
> A visionary leader
> Who sees people not as they are,
> But as all they can be!

PART III

Character Trust
(Who You Are)

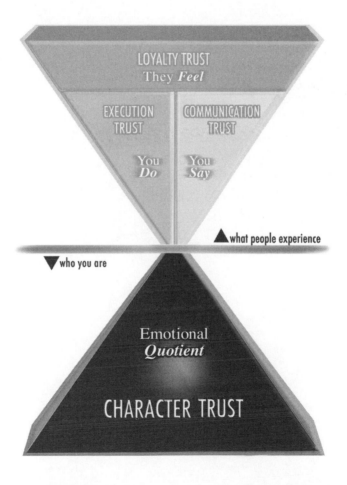

12 | Character Shapes the Leader

> *To be a great leader requires the amalgamation of many strengths, but in an age of choice there is one, character, that has a catalytic affect which helps bring out the best people have to offer.*

People followed Steve not because of his formal authority, nor because he had the backing of the second largest retailer in the world behind him (that does help though); they followed him because of his character. Remember that Lesli followed Steve to a much smaller organization, to a risky new market, and to take a demotion. Sure there are many other strengths at work in Steve. He is smart, savvy, experienced, but just like the other leaders profiled in this book, it is his character that acts like a multiplying force to help others to succeed.

Here is my definition of character: It is a set of values that drives behaviors which turn into habits or traits that shape all that you do and say. Therefore, our character is like a template or framework that shapes how people feel and respond to us, which is what I call Loyalty Trust. Inherently, character traits are behaviors that are governed by values. That is to say, character traits or habits result from first, a commitment to a set of values and second, from the ongoing effort to conform what we say and do to those values. One of the primary benefits of character is that, because these are deeper habits governed by our values, they tend to affect or infect all that we do.

When we develop the right mix of character traits, we act and communicate naturally and more effectively. Therefore, we free our minds to focus on the important problems and opportunities in front of us. Conversely, if we have weaknesses in our character because we have not developed the right values mix or formed a consistent habit structure that reflects those values, this also affects all that we do and say. Therefore, instead of focusing on business problems and opportunities, we waste a lot of time dealing with people problems or what are really trust issues.

On one level, you may readily agree with this assertion about character's importance in business. However, you may also have mixed emotions because you have seen so many managers appear to succeed in spite of weak character. Let me remind you of one of the premises of this book. Trust, and the character on which it depends, is made more critical by competitive markets and a need for a talented workforce who can choose to leave bad bosses.

Our goal in Part III is not to provide a comprehensive teaching of specific character traits, but to show how to build and use character so it permeates the way you lead. The words natural and authentic as they relate to leadership have become popular in the recent past for good reason. Leaders who work on their character create a powerful internal force that supports the two things that impact others: the way we execute and the way we communicate. People who lack a strong foundation of character must rely on less productive tactics like charisma, popularity, fear, and money to motivate. As you saw with Steve and will see later with other leaders, there are far more powerful ways to motivate or lead people that have far fewer negative side-effects. Leaders who operate from a stronger base of character are described as more authentic or natural because what they do and say resonates more naturally and powerfully with people.

An example of how you saw Steve's character impact his leadership was his high level of transparency. Another character trait that pushed up from Steve's depth of character was his directness. The various testimonials from his people revealed that they responded to his authenticity. As a result of Steve's authenticity, his people felt they could be themselves (natural) around Steve. And as we discuss more in this part, when people don't have to "put on airs" or be "guarded" they have a lot more energy and creativity to dedicate to their work.

In Part III, we will focus specifically on character traits that tend to have a significant impact on Execution, Communication, and Loyalty Trust. There are also a few traits that are misunderstood and less popular culturally, but have significant power to ignite and unite other people. As my model visually reveals, all these competencies rest on a foundation of character. Therefore, as we continue into the parts on Communication and Loyalty Trust, we will continue to reveal character traits and ideas that shape how these leaders impact people and profits.

Power of Character to Create Change

It was July 2001 and my wife and I had just spent the day hopping in and out of our realtor's Explorer in the midst of Virginia Beach's sticky, 100-degree heatwave. In our quest to find a home, we toured more houses than we could remember. It was our second house-shopping trip from our home in Pittsburgh, Pennsylvania.

The reason for the move was to get more deeply involved as volunteers in an at-risk-youth program that was doing wonderful things to keep youth out of gangs, away from drugs, and in healthy productive relationships. This nonprofit organization known as YES (Youth Entertainment Studios) put media production studios in at-risk neighborhoods around the country. Young people came to the studio's PC-based production suites to follow their passions of creating and producing music, videos, and graphics. YES was truly inspiring. Lives were being changed.

The pilot studio and small headquarters were located in the Virginia Beach/Norfolk area. The fact that these young people are making significant changes is remarkable and the central reason for that youth development goes to the heart of this book. Trust is enormously powerful in creating change.

A couple of years prior to this, my wife, three small children, and I moved into a motorhome for 18 months in order to create a character-inducing journey. We traveled the country, had a great time, and as a result began to look at life differently. One of the most meaningful things we did was spend time at YES. The result was that all of us wanted to get more involved. A couple years of inaction on our part went by before we decided to make the bold move to get involved. We needed to move to Virginia to do so. We were fortunate because my unique career permits us to live anywhere.

On this summer day, our fortitude was being tested. My wife Jill and I still had a lot of doubts about this venture, and we were frazzled by that day's house hunt.

> *When all else is in doubt, the trust in a leader's character is often the force that keeps people engaged.*

At the end of our day of house hunting, we stopped by to visit with the founder of YES, Harry Young. His office in one of the studios was in the midst of a run-down housing project that was riddled with drugs, violence, and abandonment. My wife was concerned about the prospect of our kids spending time in such a risky environment.

We were anxiously waiting for a phone call from our realtor to find out the status of an offer we had made that day. Our hopes were high when my cell phone rang and I saw that it was the realtor. The only house we visited that even remotely met our needs had gone on the market that day. We were the fifth family to do a walkthrough and the second to make an offer at the full price. The realtor informed me that we would have to sweeten the pot with an offer that was above the asking price and be willing to forgo making it contingent on a home inspection. He explained that this was common since the housing market in Virginia Beach was experiencing its greatest shortage ever.

To make matters worse, our realtor's ex-wife, who was not very fond of him, was the seller's realtor, and she would do everything she could to sway the deal to the other buyers. He was a great realtor, but this was out of his control, and he earnestly advised that even sweetening the deal might not overcome this turn of bad luck.

I got off the phone to tell Jill the bad news and my predominant thought was it's time to give up this dream. To be frank, we were already concerned that our vision of getting deeply involved in this organization was a bit unrealistic. However, there was something inside me that kept spurring me on. Much later, I realized that it was trust in Harry that kept this opportunity alive in the midst of many personal challenges that appeared to make this seem impossible.

Character in Action Is a Powerful Motivator

One of the constants I have witnessed over the years as I have worked with great leaders is that their people have no shortage of stories of how the character of the leader was a motivating force that caused them and others to endure and perform at levels that exceed their past.

Before I could tell Jill about losing the house, a former gang-banging teenager launched into a screaming tirade outside Harry's office. I was leaning against a file cabinet at an angle where I could see the anger in the body of the screaming boy. He looked like he was going to hit another young man. My eyes quickly scanned to see where our 15, 12, and 11 year-olds were relative to the mayhem. Harry was at the other side of the office and could only hear angry commotion.

I knew that Harry had a million things going on and in fact was having a very bad day. As he moved from his seat toward the door, his face revealed the mental transition he was going through internally. He was preparing himself to focus on a productive solution to this ruckus and suppressing the desire to rip into this young man.

From my vantage point, I had an eyewitness view of an amazing example of the power of trust.

Harry exited his office and came into the view of the boy doing the screaming; he said the boy's name to get his attention. The way he said his name was very important. He had this combination of firmness yet respect that reflected accurately his internal caring about this young man and the situation. I remember thinking most people would have let their tone reflect the tension of the situation and the frustration of that bad day.

The six-foot, 16 year-old boy suddenly stopped in mid-shout. This boy was previously involved in some violent fights so what happened next was quite interesting. The young man said, "Sorry, Mr. Harry." Then, as if he had just read a book about conflict management, went on to explain what he should have done. He actually said, "I know there is no excuse for me to mess everybody up in here with my screaming." His entire demeanor changed as he walked over to Harry to further explain himself.

After a brief quiet conversation with Harry, he went over to the target of his explosion, a five-foot-five boy (who looked thankful for the intervention) and worked things out without further incident. My oldest son, Joe, who had just spent a few weeks of his summer vacation with Harry, summed it up when he leaned over and whispered in my ear, "I told you! These kids really respect Harry."

As the excitement died down and we waited for Harry to return, Danene Washington, one of the founders and an adjunct professor at Norfolk State University, showed Jill and me something interesting. It demonstrated that the character and contribution my son saw in Harry was seen by others. Danene showed us an embossed invitation from the White House. The invitation was requesting that Harry attend a dinner that honored media executives and music artists for their contributions to youth development.

She did it quickly before Harry returned because he is very humble and would have disapproved of her showing us something that put him in the spotlight. Danene then excused herself to run to the bank to deposit some donations. At the top of her paperwork was a check for $25,000 from a donor who was a national news anchor personality who had worked with Harry when he was a media executive. Here was yet another person who had faith in Harry's character.

> **Witnessing trust in action is moving.**

This scene radically reinforced my thinking about our move. Instead of turning to Jill with exasperation over the house and my willingness to give up on the plan, I revealed to her the bad news as if it were a minor hurdle in our journey. I was totally inspired by what I had just seen.

For the past 20 years, I have repeatedly worked with organizations and managers whose biggest challenge was leading change. Here at YES, change was occurring that would make any manager in a corporation feel that his or her job was easy by comparison.

I remember thinking how great it would be to bring executives to spend a day at YES. If teenagers who have been abandoned, neglected, and abused can change, just think what you can do as a leader in an organization where the obstacles and baggage people bring are not nearly as substantial as what the young people at YES face.

We came back to Virginia several weeks later and spent two days in our realtor's car again and found nothing. We barely had time prior to our flight back to see one more house on the third day. We rushed through the last house in 15 minutes. As our realtor dashed us to the airport, we had him call in a bid on that last house. The plane landed and a message was waiting that the offer had been accepted. We laughed as we realized that there was much about the house we could not remember.

In the five years since that move, many friends and associates have asked how we could take such a risk when it did not include a job or financial opportunity. I tell them what I will tell you, "In hindsight, I realized that the trust I had in Harry's character was the biggest catalyst for our move."

YES, for the past 12 years, has taken the ideas it develops about engaging and developing youth and shared them with organizations all over the world. However, because of its altruistic founders, it has never built a base of financial support to help ensure its future. Our decision to move to Virginia and get involved was not because the organization was so solid that we knew it would be around for years. It was that the character of the leaders was so intense and their contribution so inspiring that we had trust in them and their vision and wanted to help them create some stability.

13 | The Power of Honesty and Integrity and the Link to Innovation

The most frequently cited combination of character traits in business is integrity and honesty. In this chapter we see how our leaders harness these critical character traits for success.

Internal Honesty Drives Better Decisions

> *Effective leaders see the world the way it is. Less effective leaders see the world the way they want it to be.*
>
> —*Peter Drucker*

Many business problems, as well as life's problems, are created or made worse by a lack of internal honesty about all aspects of a problem. Internal honesty relates to how honest we are with ourselves. It is very easy to make a business decision based on a false belief or a tainted bias. I have often heard this referred to as intellectual honesty. However, internal honesty more clearly represents my meaning in this case.

In my early twenties when I was in banking, I had a steel industry client who was in financial trouble. They pressed the bank hard to lend them more money so they could extricate themselves from the problems they were having. The bank agreed to lend the money. But as banks do, we attached a lot of strings. One string was to totally control their receivables and payables. This protected the bank's financial position by allowing us to closely monitor their cash flow.

Part of the benefit to the bank was that we would gain the additional business and the revenue from all their banking transactions by requiring them to close all their accounts with one of our competitors and open all new ones with us. When we were making the arrangements, my boss told me to set them up on all premium level services. This would increase their costs, but give us more profit. These more sophisticated cash management checking accounts had more profit margin.

I almost objected because I felt they did not need these extra services. Even though I was not on commission, deep down I understood my boss's motives and bought into them. I should have been aware that what I was doing was good for the bank but was not a good business practice for our client because it would artificially increase the cost of their doing business. I rationalized this by thinking we were doing them the favor of bailing them out of near bankruptcy with our loans to them.

I will never forget the pain I felt when the client challenged me on this decision. When I went back to the bank to change this client to the lower cost service that they should have had, the product manager told me she wanted the revenue and that the situation permitted us to make the extra profit. When I protested to my boss, he said it was not a big enough battle to fight over.

When the client got far enough out of debt that they could cut their ties to us, they cut them totally. While there were other contributing factors, I know I contributed.

The truth is, I knew it was a bad decision, and I lied to myself about the validity of other thoughts in my head that were nudging me to initially challenge my boss. My boss may have still over-ruled me, but that does not change the fact that I rationalized my actions for short-term profit and convenience. This is a specific form of lack of integrity I call *internal honesty* or in this case internal dishonesty. I learned a valuable lesson.

It is interesting to note that within one year of that incident, my boss's manager was forced to resign. The department head convened a very emotional department meeting to inform us that unethical things had been going on and that changes would be made to increase the integrity of this department. It turns out that one of the women in my group was propositioned by our boss's manager. She had the guts to speak up about it. Once she did, an avalanche of others stepped forward to share unethical conduct.

In hindsight, I have no doubt that this leader lowered the standards of the entire department, although it affords me no excuse for gouging the customer and tainting the long-term viability of the relationship. I could have done the right thing and am convinced, even if I had been fired (which is doubtful), it would have been better for the bank and my career. The other thing I noticed after this manager resigned was that the energy level of the department changed. It was noticeably different—higher. This was an example of a secondary cost of a lack of internal honesty—it diminishes energy. We'll talk more about this later.

> *We cannot be transparent with others until we are transparent with ourselves about our motives.*

Brian Cooper is the vice president of support services for CCG Systems and he has had a long-time mentor in Reggie Mano, the senior vice president of product development. Brian once said to me:

> I trust Reggie in the same way I trust Pam (the CEO). They both give it to me straight regardless of any other circumstances. I have seen times when either Pam or Reggie would be wrong on an issue and they would not hesitate to risk looking bad. They would rather tell the truth. I have seen occasions where they have made mistakes. They make no attempt to minimize the mistake. In fact, they use mistakes as learning lessons for others. But most of all, I always know they have no ulterior motives for what they do. I can trust that they always operate with the best of intentions driven by their compass of what is best for the customer.

I have worked very closely with Pam, Reggie, and Brian, and it is very interesting to note that all three have very high levels of energy. Others around CCG Systems seek them out for advice because they find that the three can use their strength of internal honesty to flush out their problems. Brian has confirmed that the internal honesty that Pam practices impacts other leaders and sets an example that pushes the culture toward greater transparency and better decision making.

With this example, I am drawing the rather obvious connection between internal honesty and candor with others (you might say external honesty). I recently gave a speech to a group of executives with a large corporation that had just gone through a series of mergers and acquisitions. There was a great deal of uncertainty and layoffs that went along with that. The CFO of this now larger corporation, made the following comment to me that makes an important point about how internal honesty doesn't guarantee external honesty. After thinking about the Radical Trust model and the value it places on candor, she said that if you are in an environment where other leaders, particularly those senior to you, are not as forthright, it is still very challenging to be as candid as you would like to be.

This relates to why we will explore more deeply the subject of candor in the next part, Communication Trust. There are more complex skills a leader often needs to be able to convey truths or insights that are contrary to accepted beliefs or practices. This is particularly relevant when others around you don't like it or are afraid of it. So I will cover candor in more depth later in the context of discussing other communication skills that can help in this process. However, there is one thing I would like to address now related to her comment.

One consistent thing I have seen with great leaders is that they work hard to ensure that the internal realizations they have transfer to other people. Another way of saying it is that these leaders have transparency between what they think and what they say, so there is very little or no difference between what they think and what they express.

In fact, these leaders avoid working with people that find it permissible to have a gap between what they think and what they say. And many of them have quit jobs and walked away from opportunities because they didn't want to bend the truth in ways that their bosses or others felt it should be bent. You might say this takes courage. And you are right. Candor takes courage. You will see more on this later. But let me give you an example of a situation that proves that internal honesty combined with candor make a leader a very valuable asset.

Honesty Is the Foundation of Problem Resolution and Strategic Thinking

Leaders who have developed internal honesty combined with a willingness to be candid about it can be feared or prized by others. Let me give you an example of how they can be prized. A highly valued trait of Radical Trust leaders is the ability to critique a problem and help peel back the layers to identify what is really going on so that accurate solutions can be applied to the real problem.

Larry Mayes, cabinet chief of human resources for the city of Boston, pioneered the installation of a YES studio in Boston. He made the following observation about Harry:

> One of the things that I have found so impressive about Harry is how his character manifests itself in a keen ability to critique a problem to a far more accurate resolution than I could come up with on my own. A lot of leaders are great at giving the command to move to resolution. But quite often they are helping others to take action on the wrong resolution.
>
> When it comes to critiquing issues where people might get emotional or upset, Harry is the embodiment of this wisdom in getting to the truth without losing people or creating walls or resentment. This trait makes anyone who works with him so much better for the experience. I call him when I go through difficult times. He always is able to sort it out and I always come away with a concrete idea.

It will be worthwhile at this point to express the difference between honesty and integrity.

Integrity is doing what you say you will do. Honesty is telling the truth.

—*Warren Bennis*

Integrity Preserves Energy

Bill Dickie sells the key component to the high-speed conveyer ovens that CiCi's Pizza uses. He met Joe Croce, CiCi's Pizza founder in the early days when it first started. Bill is still doing business with the current team that owns CiCi's Pizza.

Joe approached him early on and requested that Bill sell his company's ovens to CiCi's Pizza directly. It would reduce franchisee's investment significantly if Joe could get Bill to let him bypass the normal distributor channel. Bill said he gets that request all the time and generally doesn't do it. "You have to be pretty big and buy a lot of volume to make it worth our while to sell direct."

"I get small restaurant chains or franchises telling me all the time that we will be big some day so you should get in on the ground floor now. But for most of them, it does not happen. But Joe was consistent every time I saw him. He was driven and humble. I just knew he was going to be successful."

"I'll never forget Joe pressing me with his promise that 'if you stick with me, I'll stick with you.' I could tell Joe meant it. Seventeen years ago, Joe and I agreed to stick with each other. And he has never wavered on our relationship even though my competitor has beaten on his door repeatedly. Joe has definitely sought the best deals possible from me for his franchisees, but at the same time built a strong partnership with us that enabled us to give him tremendous pricing over a long period of time."

Bill then added, "The amazing thing to me is that Joe was able to build a company that duplicated his integrity. All those people over at CiCi's are the same. They care, they are driven, they are humble, they are great people to work with. I am amazed that since he retired three years ago, there is no noticeable decline in the company's values. How many companies can have that kind of legacy in a tough business like this?"

Bill pointed out that he felt there was a connection between Joe's integrity and his ability to maintain an extremely high energy level. "He was always upbeat and positive and I think it had a lot to do with the fact that operating out of integrity made things so much easier for Joe and CiCi's. I'd break my back for Joe, and I think a lot of people felt that way. So it made Joe's job easier."

I demonstrated with Steve how valuable truthfulness (transparency) with others is in coaching and motivating. I used my own example from banking to share with you the cost and benefit of internal honesty. I came full circle with the value Harry brings as a trusted advisor to the director of human resources of the city of Boston as a result of his internal honesty and candor (transparency). Through Joe Croce's pizza oven vendor, I demonstrated the power of integrity to enable relationships to create cost savings and profits.

This says a great deal about how we are going to teach Communication Trust. So often our own internal conflicts or lack of transparency or internal honesty prevent us from communicating effectively. Conversely, when we work at maintaining internal honesty, candor, and integrity, communicating effectively and authentically comes much easier. In Part IV, you may be surprised at how much easier it is to develop trust through the way we communicate if character is more heavily relied on than polish. But more about that later.

Radical Trust Results from Developing a Series of Character Traits

You will notice that these leaders execute, communicate, and gain loyalty through harnessing a range of character traits. For character to impact financial results, or any other kind of results, there must be an effective meshing of character traits. For example, you have probably witnessed a manager who is very candid, but lousy with internal honesty. As a result he or she diminishes respect or trust and his or her candor can be like nails on a chalkboard.

It is like the spokes of a bicycle tire. They all must have a proper tension on them to keep the tire-rim round so it can roll down the road of life more efficiently and effectively. This analogy is important because it says that first the spokes must be put in place in a balanced fashion and then tweaked repeatedly to get to a proper point of tension to make the rim round.

Bicycle enthusiasts carry a spoke tensioner (adjuster) to make corrections during their journeys in response to the dings and dents they get from uneven road surfaces. In the same way, as we hit bumps in life, we are bound to slowly or quickly develop some subtle dents in our rim. If we are not careful, these slight deviations mount up and we get "out of round" and wobble through life. Just as character is developed over time, it can also deteriorate incrementally so that its decline is not noticed until our character is so out-of-round that we derail ourselves and others, like a mini-Enron.

Some of the executives at Enron and their accounting firm Arthur D. Andersen were managers who never had enough proverbial character "spokes" to support the heavy weight of the responsibilities they accumulated. Unfortunately, they had enough talent to mask the fact that their rim was slowly getting warped. And then there were the majority who were simply the victims of these leaders' deficit in character.

One of the reasons Harry's character impacted my family so much is that, more than any other person I have had the privilege to see upclose, he has developed the widest range of character traits to a high level. I have known him for 26 years.

This is directly associated with why he was able to lead in Hollywood and also why he has been able to innovate in the very challenging at-risk-youth sector. He has navigated the complex world of education, churches, and government to develop very productive relationships, initiatives, and results.

Ironically, Harry's openness about his diligence to work at character has been a powerful trait that has caused most people that work with him to realize that the achievement of high-functioning character requires the mastery of numerous character traits. That, for many, has been a source of inspiration.

> *Being transparent about our effort to develop our character becomes a powerful source of instruction to others.*

Once again, here is an observation from Larry Mayes about how Harry as a leader impacts character:

> I love this guy so much. . . . To know this guy who is supporting a neighborhood of kids on his own pushes you to examine yourself.
>
> To be in his presence, to know him is to be arrested. Specifically, his willingness to be open and "self critical" is one thing that makes him so effective. The word arresting comes to mind because his impact on people is so significant. If not for the fact for having my family and commitments here in Boston, I would be there in Virginia Beach working with him. His character is contagious and it raises others to a higher standard!

As you read more about how these Radical Trust leaders are so successful, you will repeatedly see that it is not the perfection of any one trait that is the reason for their success, but the sustaining and strengthening of a set of character traits working in concert.

14

Importance of Character and Emotional Intelligence in Development

Unfortunately, while most people agree that character is critical to leadership and trust, many people and organizations are not open about the personal effort required to maintain or build character. A false perception has developed that it is a sign of weakness to reveal that you as a leader have areas of your character that you need to develop. However, this perception is beginning to change.

In the past 15 years, we have seen many organizations add character traits as core values in the hopes that employees would adapt and practice traits such as integrity. That, by the way, is the most commonly referenced corporate character trait or core value in organizations today.

A few organizations have begun to tie their incentive and reward systems to core values. Many years ago prior to the communications conglomerate Marconi folding into Ericsson, they made the bold move to tie compensation to core values. I was privileged to be minimally involved as a consultant in the very early stages.

While I am not going to show you how to tie compensation to character, I am going to show you the most effective way to get others to adapt character traits that are good for business and people. And that is why relationships are so critical to helping others develop character.

> *There is constant pressure that causes many people to choose what appears to be a shortcut and what inevitably is really a sacrifice of integrity.*

It takes time to grow character and, as leaders, we must be willing to place positive tension on the subtle things that lead to stronger character. In the past 10 years, a field of study that is consistent with what I am expressing here has become popular.

Emotional Intelligence for Leaders

Emotional intelligence quotient (EQ) is a concept that has become popular in business at around the same time character and trust began to become more relevant. Emotional intelligence quotient is also referred to as emotional quotient. The omission of the word intelligence is purposeful to avoid confusion with intelligence quotient (IQ) which some believe is genetic and limited in its ability to grow in adults.

By this point, you have concluded that this book is based on the idea that character can be developed. Most leaders I know will confess that they were not born leaders but that they developed into leaders. However, there is a school of thought that says character and leadership are born and are not developed. So as not to get bogged down in that debate, I am going to move on by saying that the evidence in this book is on the side of believing EQ, character, and, therefore, leadership are all learned and can be developed.

But let me explain how the concept of EQ has added to the modern thinking about character. On a simple level, EQ has become known as the ability to manage your emotions in such a way that they support your success instead of detracting from it. For example, a manager with high EQ instead of becoming volatile when challenged by a subordinate will engage and diffuse in a productive fashion.

Many people believe the term was first used by Carl Lans in a Dutch book in the 1960s. But most credit David Goleman with applying the term to business in his 1995 book, *Emotional Intelligence* (New York: Bantam, 2005).

The term *emotional intelligence* resonated with people when they would describe how some people seemed to be deficient (immature) in their ability to deal with conflict at work. Thus, EQ became relevant to management selection because people who do not handle conflict well usually are not good management candidates. Emotional quotient also appealed to people in describing deficiencies that many people had dealing with stressful times of change. It has become common to say that people with low EQ are more likely to let their emotions cause them to resent or rebel against embracing new processes or strategies. Therefore, many organizations hire consultants or trainers or develop internal curriculum to help them elevate management and employee EQ prior to engaging in change.

In each case that the word EQ was used, you could substitute character in its place. For my purposes related to building trust, they are synonymous. Both require a person to deal with the same deeper belief systems and behaviors in order to develop. Another way of saying this is that developing character or higher EQ requires a person to examine what he or she values and be willing to rearrange the way he or she thinks.

> *Success with character or EQ first requires the shifting of values, then the change of behaviors, and perhaps the addition of skill development.*

Character and EQ are different than competencies such as execution and communication because issues related to character or EQ are much more deeply rooted in our paradigms and habits. By paradigm, I mean your view of the world. Your paradigm is the historical way you look at things and value them based on your life experiences and knowledge.

Character and EQ have more to do with altering your belief systems. Once the core beliefs are genuinely altered, then actions and words flow more naturally from them. The real challenge is in getting people to realize they need to deal with the root issues such as shifting their values. This book may appear altruistic at times because we so often drill deep into values. However, the economic facts and case studies indicate that it is not altruism alone that makes these ideas powerful.

You will notice that many of the stories in this book that are designed to teach character are aimed at creating an "ah-hah" and are designed to validate and elevate the importance of the subject matter in your mind. That is why I am careful to provide real proof of the business value of each lesson on character. Let me give you a couple more practical examples of important character traits as they relate to our emotions.

Character, Emotions, and Values

Take humility for example. The most important challenge of mastering humility is to get an arrogant person to rearrange his core values to reduce his self-importance. The toughest part about that is to convince him it is in his self-interest to do so. That is a big value or paradigm shift. Many people's paradigm is warped when it comes to this because popular culture teaches that confidence and arrogance can be the same thing; or worse that self-love is the same thing as self-indulgence. Once you learn that self-love does not need to include indulgence or that you can be confident without being arrogant, you are empowered. More simply, you have gone through a paradigm shift that improves your character.

Therefore, to grow character or EQ, people must be willing to open up their value system and be willing to make multiple adjustments. For example, here is yet another values shift overly confident managers need to make if humility is going to take root. Valuing others and being more honest, particularly as it relates to taking credit for things, are critical if you are going to become more humble.

Or here is another aspect of EQ related to the negative impact of emotions: If we lose emotional control, we reduce our ability to be trusted. That is why you will see *consistency in attitude* listed as an important character/EQ trait.

Also there is the idea that managers need to be sensitive to their constituent's emotions. A manager needs to be able to read people's emotions so he or she can react more effectively. Many of our employees, customers, and vendors may not be as emotionally mature and may not process their emotions effectively. So leaders who can "read" people well have an advantage in better understanding and reacting to people. You will see examples of how these leaders do this.

A good leader can read emotions and then react in ways that help. A basic example is that a good manager will respond more effectively to a hysterical, ranting employee by avoiding the common response that escalates the situation by yelling back. You will see *values others* also listed as an important character trait in many organizations. An emotionally mature person is better able to value others.

Therefore, my use of the word *character* references what some refer to as emotional traits that leaders can and should develop. Many of the problems managers have are a direct result of emotional immaturity. One of the important aspects of the discussion surrounding emotional intelligence is that it has caused the business world to embrace the idea that it is a good investment to challenge people to grow emotionally.

I have had many people approach me after my speeches on Radical Trust and say, "This is just like EQ." Or "Is there a difference between what you are talking about and EQ?"

For example, people use EQ when they refer to employees of a hospital who are not buying into change. They might say, "Our employees have been through so much with cost-cutting and personnel cuts that we need to help them collectively boost their EQ right now." But if they refer to a burned out hospital administrator as being a source of problems, they tend to say, "That leader doesn't have the character to handle the magnitude of these problems." Emotional intelligence quotient has had a tendency to be used to talk about developing the character of employees. However, character tends to be the word I hear most often when people talk about developing leaders.

Therefore, since the growth in EQ is consistent with the development of character as a business issue, I want to make sure to validate them being the same for my purposes.

From this point forward, to keep things simple, I use the term *character* and not EQ. However, remember that in this context I am using character synonymously with EQ.

Four Fundamentals to Build and Sustain Character

1. Hire for Character

Make character central to what you look for when hiring managers. I was speaking at a conference a year ago and David Snyder, the author of *How to Mind Read Your Customers* (New York: Amacom, 2001), approached me after my talk. He asked if he could cite some of my ideas on leadership and trust in his upcoming book, *How to Hire a Champion* (New York: Career Press, scheduled release: fall of 2007). David, who now leads the executive recruitment practice at Headway Corporate Resources, a national staffing and human capital resources company, explained how he and Headway had pioneered methods to screen and hire leaders based on character. I went to David's session at that conference and heard him discuss the value of how their selection methods incorporate character assessment in the hiring process.

This is yet another case-in-point that validates my assertion that trust and the character necessary for it are no longer just nice to have. They are more critically important for business success than ever. Headway and others are proving that it is becoming a mainstream hiring practice.

The first step is to ensure your formal hiring process includes screening for the character traits that are important for your business. You should do this by insuring that the interview process includes questions about specific character traits you need. Remember that not only is the interview process about screening a candidate, it also sets the expectations about what you want from associates and tells candidates about the values of your culture.

You also may want to use assessment tools to help determine the character of an applicant. As I mentioned before, the popular language used today is EQ. So if you are looking for character assessment tools, you may want to search under character and/or Emotional Quotient assessments. You will also find a hiring assessment tool at my site: www.joehealey.com/radicaltrust.htm.

This goes back to the movement that has organizations adding character traits to their core values. By identifying the behavior you expect, you greatly increase the likelihood it will occur. Like goal setting, the more specific we are, the more likely it is that specific character traits you want will be reflected in the way your people do business.

2. Teach by Example

The best way to inculcate character into an organization is for leaders to exemplify it every day. I will share with you some amazing stories that demonstrate how a leader who acts with consistent character becomes a powerful tool to manifest character growth in others.

3. The Mix Is Critical

I would like to expound on what I mentioned in the last chapter. Character traits work in harmony like ingredients in a good sauce. For example, I am sure you have met managers who are humble, but who are also not transparent or less than honest. Their humility has very little ability to make a positive impact.

In fact, the old saying, "too much of a good thing" can be a problem with overemphasizing certain character traits. One of the destructive things I have seen is people making the mistake of assuming that because they are strong in one area of character, they are in good shape. For example, some managers think that because they have high integrity, they can accost and intimidate people with their metrics or criticism. I have seen so many managers surprised when they don't get the results they want from their people. And they say, "But I was just honest-with them." Meanwhile their subordinates are saying, "He is an arrogant . . ."

This tendency to be top-heavy with a few character traits and light in others is very common and destructive. And like education, most people stop developing their character once they get into their twenties and often long before that. But if you study great leaders, you will find that they are lifelong students of both knowledge and specifically character development.

4. Keep the Pressure On

You may recall that Ben Franklin worked hard to master his 13 virtues. His book on the subject, Benjamin Franklin's *The Art of Virtue* was re-published in 1996 (edited by George L. Rogers, Eden Prairie, MN: Acorn Publishing, 1996). He would work on one virtue at a time until he mastered it and then move on to work on the next. But the key is that when he mastered the thirteenth, he started back on the first. Ben Franklin gave voice to the fact that we tend to backslide and need on-going maintenance. His practice of constantly cycling through the virtues enabled him to create a harmony or a melding together of these virtues.

This leads me to the next important principle: the idea that you must accept the reality that you will always need to be working on your character. I call this keeping tension on character.

Great Character Requires Positive Tension

When I say that strong character requires constant positive tension some people get a look of relief, and tell me that in our microwave society, there is this false expectation that you deal with it once and then your character is fixed.

There is a principle I have been teaching for many years that leaders seem to appreciate. It is the idea that there are certain character traits that come easier than others depending on your personality and your background. For example, folks born during the Depression tended to be better with fiscal discipline. People who have had painful failure in their lives tend to find it easier to be humble.

People who have been shunned because of how they look or how much they don't have, tend to value others more easily or go to the other extreme and have to deal with jealousy. So most of us find some character traits come easily, while others are more difficult to master. You could say that humility or honesty seems more natural to some people, and you might say that some people with whom you have had the displeasure of working seemed to be born liars. But I guarantee that you and everybody else has some trait with which they struggle. And those can be the ones that hold us back.

When I used the word positive tension earlier, I was referring to the need to be concisely aware of what our character weaknesses are and temper them. Of course, what really helps with this is when you tell others to keep you "in-check."

I am sure you have seen this in practice with high-functioning teams. People on the team hold each other accountable and are open about some of the flaws others have; especially character flaws. This occurs where there is high candor, transparency, and accountability with each other. When this exists we say that the team has camaraderie or esprit de corps.

Unfortunately, most cultures have a tendency to make giving feedback about character flaws, inappropriate or uncomfortable. The reason is that many cultures have conformed to the myth that character can't change. So some corporate cultures have reluctance to make discussing character traits part of the review process. "People will be insulted."

In fact, that is one reason that many organizations have made character traits part of their core values. It validates their importance and underscores the need to be diligent about developing character. It also opens the door for people to address character shortcomings in reviews and other forums. Often it is just a matter of how you couch it and what words you use that can help others to be receptive to your coaching about character traits.

A great way for a leader to help himself, an individual or a whole team is to have an open dialogue about character. There is a free outline for a one-on-one coaching session at my web site:

www.joehealey.com/radicaltrust.htm. There is also an outline you can use to facilitate a team discussion and an in-depth assessment you and your team can use to provide more in-depth feedback and accountability. Of course, by permitting your people to evaluate you, you open the door for them to be more receptive to you giving them candid feedback.

The key to keeping some of your character flaws from undermining the trust you build is to be open about them and continually willing to place tension on them. Some of the best leaders I know admit their flaws to their people and give them permission to challenge them. And when they are challenged, they react with appreciation. This in and of itself is incredibly empowering to your team.

15

Valuing Others Creates a Culture of Success

If you call CiCi's Pizza's distribution company, JMC Restaurant Distribution, you are likely to connect with Sue Tinsley's inviting personality. Her role of being a primary go-to person for franchisees caused the president of the company, Bob Kulick, to give her the title of director of first impressions. In everything Sue does, it is evident that she is invested in this company. If you ask a franchisee about her, they will say they love her and that she makes them feel like family. They will tell you that she is that way 24/7.

Children who feel valued perform better. And so do adults!

This chapter deals with the idea that leaders who value people get higher levels of performance from them. So I am going to tell you the story behind Sue that supports and encourages her to be all that she can be. Sue is the way she is because the cultural character of CiCi's Pizza has encouraged in her a deep sense of appreciation and respect for other people.

A company can go to the expense of giving an employee any number of perks that say thanks. But if this is a one-time gesture from a manager who is generally too busy to care about the employee, the money spent on the perk is probably a waste. Conversely, a simple thank you or conversation with an employee about her family from a manager who really values her, will do far more than a catalog full of employee perks.

It is interesting to note that not one of the leaders profiled in this book uses gimmicks to make people feel valued. They do not do "employee of the month." In fact, Joe says, "I hate that cookie-cutter stuff." But every one of these leaders makes people feel so valued that their employee retention is higher, their ability to draw out talent is magnified, and they get amazing effort and innovation from their people.

The reason is revealed in this story that proves that great leaders work at a deeper level, the character level, to value people. This is a lifestyle, not a "to do" on a priority list.

Valuing People Increases Discretionary Effort

CiCi's Pizza made a decision several years ago to do some fund raising for an at-risk-youth program called Happy Hill Farm. They were just shy of their goal of raising $20,000. Sue heard about the shortfall and quietly put the difference on the desk of the manager who was running the campaign. She didn't want anyone else to know that she enabled them to make their goal. However, they did figure out she did it.

She did not want any strings attached to her contribution and did not want any attention. Her knowledge that she helped out was enough. I find great leaders to be like this. When great leaders do things to personally help people, they do it as a real contribution. They don't pretend they are being benevolent while attaching strings or seeking recognition. They do know that they are making an investment that will yield a dividend, but they don't force the yield or seek notoriety for giving.

When I told Sue I knew about how much she valued people at CiCi's, she immediately said, "Oh Joe, that's part of who we are here." And then she went on to tell me about the day the president of the company gave her a car. Sue told me the following:

> I had been working at CiCi's for two or three years, and had grandchildren in a town a couple hours away. I drove to see them every weekend. I had an old Blazer that was not in good shape. I came in one Monday morning and Bob Kulick was not there. Elissia Defoor, the vice president of customer success took me out to the parking lot and handed me the keys to a Mazda. I was stunned. Then she handed me the title. I know Bob wasn't there on purpose because he didn't want to make a big deal over it.

I am sharing this conversation with Sue because I called to interview someone else at the office and happened to tell her I was featuring Joe Croce in a book about trust. Sue said, "You have picked the right person and the right company." She went on to tell me the story about the car and the following ones as well. She was so passionate as she told me: "Three years ago, my mom died. She was 90 years old and had a good life. We were very close and it broke my heart. I was at work when I got the call. One of the other folks in the office called Bob on his cell. He was on his way to a dental appointment. He immediately turned around and came and held me and grieved with me. He took me home and we sat and reminisced about my mom."

Before I could say anything, Sue headed right into another example of valuing people through generosity:

There is a wonderful man, named Ed Shipman, who has dedicated his life and home to taking care of kids whose parents are on drugs or in prison. Dr. Phil profiled Mr. Shipman, the founder of Happy Hill Farm, on his show. Mr. Shipman stopped by the office one day to thank Bob for our support of his kids. Mr. Shipman noticed the new office furniture Bob had just gotten from an Amish man who handmakes furniture. He particularly commented on the unique standing desk where Bob had his computer. Mr. Shipman is in his eighties now and suffers from bad arthritis in his back. Bob gave him the phone number of the Amish man so he could look into getting a desk like his.

Bob later found out that Mr. Shipman could not get one. So Bob asked one of our drivers to take his desk out to Happy Hill Farm and give it to Mr. Shipman. I said to Bob, "but you loved that desk." He said, "Anything I can do to keep Mr. Shipman moving is a good investment. He needs to be here."

> **The ability to value people is the result of developing the character trait of generosity.**

When I asked Bob about these stories, he shrugged them off and went to talk about what Sue did that made a difference at CiCi's. He then connected Sue's contribution to Joe by sharing stories about how he witnessed Joe's demonstration of valuing and respecting people. Bob shared how Joe Croce had personally loaned the money to cover the total cost of both capital and the franchise fee for a franchisee. He further explained that the culture they have created and sustained was fueled by a leader demonstrating with actions a deeply felt desire to value people with a spirit of generosity.

Here are some of Joe's thoughts about valuing people. He felt that a primary issue in showing people that you value them is how you listen to them: "I listened, understood, and responded because I cared. I fired some people who would not listen to the input of others, or sometimes they would not respond appropriately to others. It is critical to understand and respect other people."

Joe believes that a "classless" corporate culture is critical to people developing into the best they can be. He feels firmly that it is his obligation as part of valuing his people to remind himself and anyone else that forgets that: "I never looked at someone based on the amount of money they made. I work to treat every paid employee as if they are volunteering."

Joe reveals that leaders need to do things with their employees "that let you get to know them and understand more deeply the value they bring." It is not about being as good or better than them. It is not about showing them that you are willing to do the lowly work. Joe added, "It is about spending time with them and understanding better what they do, so your decisions reflect them." This enabled Joe to better assess people's talents so, "I get the right people on the right seats on the bus."

Many new franchisees said CiCi's was the best weight-loss program. Many lost 20 to 30 pounds because it was the first time they were happy in years.

—Joe Croce

One of the great stories Bob told me about Joe was this:

Joe liked to stay in touch with how our distribution worked and loved to get to know our employees. So after spending the entire day dealing with CEO issues, he put on jeans and a T-shirt and climbed in a truck at midnight with a driver. They made deliveries until 5:00 A.M. when the driver accidentally punched in the wrong alarm code at one of the restaurants where they were making a delivery.

The police came and were questioning the driver who took them over to the truck where a perspiring, Joe Croce was loading a 100-pound bag of flour on a two-wheeled dolly. The driver tried to explain that they were not thieves and pointed out that the guy up there was the president and founder of CiCi's. The police officer laughed and said, "Yeah, and I am the chief of police."

It took some further proof to satisfy the officer. Most people would react the way the police officer did, that is to say that we are conditioned to believe once a person climbs the ladder to a lofty leadership slot, they are above some things. However, in the same way that most people would not believe that the president would be unloading flour in the back of a truck at 5:00 in the morning, most people when exposed to a leader like Joe react with appreciation and respect.

It is important to note that I am not advocating that leaders need to do menial or manual labor to prove they care or are in touch with their people. This may not be right for some leaders in some situations. And in some cases, leaders can send the wrong message by trying to please their people and become popular. The point is that Joe felt this would be a good way to stay in touch with his people and it was a critical part of the operation. There was no attempt to gain popularity, but there was a true spirit of respect for this hard work and a genuine desire to pitch in. And that is what people at CiCi's responded to in Joe.

Just as people have discretionary money to spend, they have discretionary effort to invest. You can bet that this driver, like others at

CiCi's, invested a lot more of their discretionary effort to make that company successful because of Joe.

Joe understands that we live in a world that communicates through various mediums. With over 500 franchise locations when he was president, it was certainly hard to connect with all the franchisees, employees, and vendors as he would have liked. Bob said, "But the one thing he always did, was maximize one-on-one time when he could get it. We would be at conferences and Joe was always taking people aside to have private conversations with them. That tendency, although simple, and maybe only lasting a couple of minutes, made it very clear that that person was valued and counted."

Joe said, "I found it critical to get as much face-time as I could with all our people be they franchisees, employees, or vendors. I found making that extra effort gave my relationships a real boost."

Joe was on the road visiting franchises and the last one he visited was in the midst of the dinner rush. Joe knew he could not distract them from dinner customers. He jumped in and helped serve; observing and chatting up a storm. It was 1:30 A.M. by the time he got out of there. And the employees watched in amazement as he walked over to his inexpensive compact rental car to make the three-hour drive to the next city.

When I asked Joe about the rental car, he simply said, "My motto was, we will not spend money on things that don't benefit our people or guests." Sounds a lot like Sam Walton. Joe said:

> People have to know that you value them. If we don't value them and we make bad business decisions, it will cost us dearly in trust. And people are always watching. In this age, you can't fake it. People are smart. As soon as they see a leader with double standards or fake agendas, they ask themselves: "How can I trust that person?" People knew I valued them not because I wanted to make it look that way. But because I learned that it is easy and fun and it works extremely well in running a business.

Joe would frequently deny press interviews to avoid looking like he made CiCi's what it was. He really felt, and still feels, that it was a "we," not a "me." Joe said, "People rallied around the belief that nobody is better than anybody else."

Soon after interviewing Bob Kulick, he sent me an e-mail with the following note about Joe and the power of valuing people:

> This is the CiCi's training department's quote of the week. It is a good way to cap off the discussion about Joe. Mark Twain summed up why people are attracted to him: "Keep away from people who try to belittle your ambitions. Small people always do that, but the really great make you feel that you, too, can become great."

Character Is the Bridge from Entrepreneur to CEO

Joe Flanigan, chief marketing officer of Gold's Gym, worked with Joe at CiCi's as the chief marketing officer for many years and made the following observation of how Joe's character equipped him to successfully navigate from entrepreneur to CEO. (I'll refer to Joe Flanigan as Mr. Flanigan so as not to confuse you when I refer to Joe Croce as Joe.) Mr. Flanigan said, "It was amazing to watch Joe's evolution from hard-driving entrepreneur who built a small business, to a CEO of a major franchise and leader of men. He always had the 'come follow me' magnetism. But he chiseled his character to transition from a great entrepreneur to a great leader. He could communicate with small franchise owners where CiCi's was their first venture to sophisticated, major players in the restaurant business such as the former president of Pizza Hut who ended up buying 12 CiCi's franchises."

Mr. Flanigan voiced that part of why Joe transitioned from entrepreneur to CEO so successfully when so many others failed was his humility. "Because he was humble, he was able to be a great student. He was a sponge, a learner." Mr. Flanigan, as the chief marketing officer, had to prepare Joe for the big-time, so to speak. As CiCi's began to use media for advertising, its sheer size meant the media was also beating on CiCi's door. "Joe knew nothing about media and very quickly he began to grasp the complex issue related to TV station ratings, print advertising, PR campaigns, and so on. He was never uncomfortable being the student. I have seen many other senior executives get uncomfortable when you spoke about topics outside of their expertise. Not Joe. He just kept asking me to feed him more and more."

"I enjoyed having my office near his. I learned a great deal just by being close to him. I carried so much from Joe. He permanently filled me with a unique high-energy hands–on sense of urgency. To this day many years later, I still am thankful about how Joe impacted my style of leadership and energy."

Character Is the Fuel for Speed and Passion

Have you ever been in a Wal-Mart early in the morning and seen the employees chanting? They do a chant that would remind most people of what an excited group of high school athletes do before a game to pump themselves up. This may not be your cup of tea, and I must confess that it is not mine, but I reserved judgment because of my great respect for Sam Walton. I knew from researching him that he chanted with great authenticity and energy.

I came to more fully respect this when I was at a CiCi's annual franchise meeting and saw a room full of former executives, blue-collar workers, and everyone in between do the same kind of cheer. I knew these people meant it. Some were millionaires as a result of CiCi's; others were just starting out, but all did it because they loved raising the energy in the room as if they were going into an important game. In today's fast-paced world, high energy is critical. Leaders are constantly looking for ways to elevate the energy of a team or community.

The character traits we are talking about in this chapter are what give you permission to raise the energy level. That was certainly true of Sam Walton, and it is what Mr. Flanigan saw at CiCi's and took with him.

Mr. Flanigan also believes that the real reason it takes longer to engage some people into a higher speed of acceptance is they have been burned by low-trust leaders in the past who did the song and dance, but did not have the substance behind it. It is like the high school football team that failed to practice, but was good at doing the chant before the game. Pretty soon people start to blame the chant instead of the void behind it.

Mr. Flanigan knows that given the state of low trust that exists in the workplace, leaders have to accept that people need time to figure them out. You have to accelerate the time it takes your people to warm up to you by ensuring that the people you allow to surround you have strong character. A leader who is great at execution and getting lots of things done can be counterproductive to speed in the long-run if his or her character impedes others from buying in.

This subject of buy-in brings up a critical issue. And that is the concept of restoring trust when it is strained or broken. By this point, it may have occurred to you that the character traits we have been discussing (internal honesty, candor, integrity, humility, gratitude, generosity, and valuing of others) reduce or prevent broken trust. And it is these same traits that make restoring trust much easier.

Later when we talk about Communication Trust it will become more apparent that the same character traits and communication skills we use to build trust are what we use to restore it. It is accurate to say that these leaders have very few relationships where trust has been strained or broken. And where that did occur, it did not remain long because the mastery of these competencies inherently equips us to be able to more effectively restore trust when it is broken.

16 | Gauging Character for Decision Making

There are numerous critical points in any leader's career where he has to make a decision that hinges on trust in one or two people with whom he has not had the luxury of knowing long. This relates to decisions about other leaders in your organization whom you don't know, vendors, and the career moves you will make. I am sure you or someone you know has made a choice based on the same perception I had of Harry. He is a stand-up person you can count on. However, unlike my decision with Harry, you later find yourself mired in a bad situation because the people in whom you trusted just were not who you thought they were. And unfortunately, in today's world of internal matrix management and external vendor partnerships, our bad judgment about someone else's character can come back to diminish our reputation.

Engaging in Relationships with Low-Trust People Can Be Costly

I was burned once by the president of a U.S. subsidiary of a U.K.-based firm who needed a company turned around in Kansas. I didn't want to move my wife and three small kids that far from our roots on the East Coast at that time in our lives. But he made some big promises and did a great job of displaying trustworthiness to a still somewhat naive 30 year-old. The deal we struck was that I would take over as general manager of one of his troubled subsidiaries for about a year to turn it around and then I would replace one of the retiring presidents of one of his more stable companies in a location that better suited my family.

The first sign of a problem was when he reneged on some terms of our agreement soon after I moved. It was a relatively small issue of a company car. The company made a decision to stop paying for its executives' cars in the United States. However, since it was part of my compensation package that was specifically negotiated by the headhunter, integrity would dictate that this president should have felt bound to at least have a conversation with me about it.

I had a good package and have always been a team player and would have forgone that perk for the sake of the team. However, the news came in a form letter with a note scribbled on it next to his signature that said, something like: "Sorry, I forgot we were implementing this policy when we negotiated the terms of your contract."

The short version of the story is that within three months, I had every out-of-line cost at this company back on track, had increased sales, and had the company performing well again. But the kicker came a few months later during the first week of the new year when this guy's assistant called my treasurer and asked her to backdate sales receipts to the previous year. We all knew this guy was getting a bonus for U.S. sales and knew exactly why he was asking. I ended my tenure with them when I spoke up about the issue.

In hindsight, I realize it was easy to turn this company around in three months because this low-character president had a lot of incompetent people who were busy milking their positions as he did instead of building value. So cleaning up their messes was not all that hard. The biggest problems at this company were labor cost and quality. Both of these were tied to the horrible morale that existed. And all of these were tied directly to a lack of trust that was rampant in this company. Greater diligence could have avoided this bad deal.

How to Verify Character

Let me share with you a different story that illustrates how you ensure that you partner with people who are more likely to deliver what they promise.

Joe Flanigan, whom you met in Chapter 15, was a senior executive at PepsiCo in Orlando. A headhunter called him to recruit him because a 90-store franchise chain, CiCi's Pizza, was in a heavy growth mode and needed a public relations and marketing expert to help them. Mr. Flanigan politely told the headhunter that he was not interested in working for a small business even if it was growing in leaps and bounds.

Joe loved what he saw on Mr. Flanigan's resume and, told the headhunter to tell Mr. Flanigan that he would meet him in any airport in the country during his travels to spend some time with him to pitch his vision. They met at the Atlanta airport in Delta's Crown Room during one of Mr. Flanigan's layovers. The brief meeting turned into a couple of hours and a few weeks later Mr. Flanigan was in the summer heat of Texas riding in Joe's convertible visiting stores.

Mr. Flanigan was catching the vision. Instead of his corporate eyes seeing a risky small business, he saw a rapidly growing 90-location franchise business with a business model primed for growth. Mr. Flanigan had three small kids back in Orlando, Florida, and he told Joe that he would have to guarantee his $150,000 salary and part of the quarterly bonuses that would be part of his compensation. Joe agreed to pay him for three years if things didn't work out.

Joe told him that he would put it in writing, but that in six months Mr. Flanigan would want to throw out the contract because it would prevent him from making what Joe wanted him to make—which was even more.

Mr. Flanigan had the offer he wanted that would compensate for the risk of leaving a blue-chip career at PepsiCo and uprooting his family. But with a small business like this, Mr. Flanigan realized that even with a contract, he may not have a guarantee of security. He knew the contract was worthless if Joe was not the man he portrayed. On reflection, this line of thinking was causing Mr. Flanigan to think he would not take the deal.

As that day in the convertible progressed, Mr. Flanigan found the key to what is needed when you have to make a decision with a lot of potential and a lot of risk that hinges on a leader's word. The answer came through several conversations Mr. Flanigan had with people during that day.

As they visited stores, Mr. Flanigan met one franchise owner after another who had stories about Joe and CiCi's. Twelve years later, as Mr. Flanigan shared this with me, he said he could still remember it like it was yesterday: "I was meeting people who had turned their lives over to CiCi's Pizza. This restaurant business and the financial investment was a serious life commitment. Everyone had admiration for Joe. They were frank with me in saying 'you can leap and you will be all right.'"

"One franchise owner I met that day told me how he used to be the repairman for the company who sold CiCi's their pizza ovens. This man talked passionately about Joe. 'Let me tell you about Joe Flanigan; when I use to be in the oven repair business, I came out at all hours day and night to fix Joe's ovens.'"

Mr. Flanigan interrupted the story to say, "George was 45 then when he made his decision and also had a lot of risk in getting into the franchise game. George said that Joe was always very respectful and appreciative. One time when Joe thanked him, George told him it was his goal to buy a CiCi's restaurant. 'If you are all wearing out these ovens this quick, you have to be making serious money. I will come to you when I have the money.'"

And Mr. Flanigan said with a smile in his voice, "Now here I was nine years after George made his decision sitting in one of George's CiCi's locations in Irving, Texas, that did over one million dollars in sales that year." At this point in the story, Joe was in the back talking to a cook. George looked at the open door where Joe was and smiled at Mr. Flanigan and said with a nod toward Joe, "That guy loaned me the down-payment. And he has long since been paid back with my profits."

Mr. Flanigan laughed as he said to me, "Wait till you hear this one. At another location, I met Frank Rogers who had three units at that point. He had this warm southern drawl that spoke of humility and simplicity. Ironically, he used to be a driver who delivered Coke to CiCi's. He told me, 'I went to my father-in-law to borrow the money and I joined Joe in the business.'" Frank didn't say it, but Mr. Flanigan was able to figure out that Frank had become a millionaire because of his trust in Joe. Mr. Flanigan said he encountered story after story as he visited franchises and the offices of CiCi's Pizza.

Mr. Flanigan went back to Orlando and moved his family, not just because he trusted Joe. He hardly knew Joe. But, as a businessman, Mr. Flanigan knew that if this many successful people were working hard and investing their savings and reputation in CiCi's then he could trust CiCi's, too. Mr. Flanigan knows that if you lack personal history the best way to gauge if you can trust a leader's character is to take note of the people that choose to surround the leader you are seeking to trust.

17 | Fiscal Discipline Creates Opportunity

In October 2003, Joe Flanigan and I sat in the audience with 500 CiCi's franchise owners and watched grown people cry as Joe Croce gave his farewell speech. He decided to retire at age 44 and sold the company to a group of employees who would carry on. I was to provide a motivational keynote on leadership for this annual franchise meeting, and I came early so that I could hear the president's comments.

One of the great benefits of my work is that I get to listen to some very wise leaders share their insights. I am in the habit of taking notes on some of the things they share. But on this day, as Joe spoke, I was bowled over. This guy was incredible.

His 90-minute talk focused almost wholly on the importance of character in business. As I looked around the room, these hard-driving restaurateurs were nodding their heads in agreement. Then came the grand finale. They had an open-microphone session after Joe's talk so that franchisees had an opportunity to get up and say some words to Joe. That went on for over an hour. All around the room were people with tears in their eyes.

I made my presentation two hours later, missed my flight home, and was very thankful the open-microphone session separated me from Joe's talk. He was one incredibly tough act to follow. During Joe's talk, he emphasized fiscal discipline as being key to giving him the freedom to be successful.

Joe Croce feels that if he had failed to master fiscal discipline, he would not have been as successful a leader or, ironically, as successful in amassing a personal financial fortune.

Your Lifestyle May Cost You a Better Life

Joe's farewell talk was a summary of what he felt were the most important practices that enabled him and CiCi's Pizza to be so successful. At 44, Joe was retiring as a multimillionaire. He had helped to make many people financially independent and was leaving a company in great fiscal shape that would go on to create several more millionaires.

The point that Joe emphasized the most during his talk was this: If you are going to run a business, you have to pay attention to the numbers. You have to be a good steward of the resources you have. Sometimes you are flush and sometimes you have to make things work with a tight cash flow. But more than anything else, your own fiscal soundness will impact your ability to lead.

Joe did not mince words. He said he has heard and seen a lot of failures that stemmed directly from a leader's inability to manage his personal finances. Joe gave this simple formula: "I am very thankful I learned early in my career to live on only 70 percent of what I made.

I have practiced the habit of giving 10 percent to God, I save 10 percent, and I have another 10 percent to use as a cushion, give away, or use on more risky investments."

Joe went on to explain that people think this sounds crazy in this day and age, but he said the incredible freedom that comes from this approach gave him much more room to navigate life. He openly said that many talented people get stuck in jobs that are wrong for them because they are mortgaged to the hilt. "Most people can't afford to take advantage of some great business opportunities that come their way because they have no reserve."

And then Joe got emphatic and said that the strain of living under financial pressure stifles most leaders' ability to dream big and create large visions. He said that both entrepreneurs and their counterparts in senior leadership positions in large corporations were not much different than the average American in the way they embraced far too much debt in their personal lives. Joe said, "A lot of leaders are good at masking the financial pressure that limits their options. But failing to recognize the cost of that stress is draining their energy."

Joe challenged the audience by saying, "People tell me 'I can't possibly live on only 70 percent of what I make. I would be giving up far too much in terms of lifestyle.'"

He then refuted that by pointing out that most people never weigh the cost of all that financial stress on their future. He said with great emphasis, "I know for a fact I never would have succeeded in this business if I allowed my thinking to be warped by the typical financial pressure businesspeople endure in their home lives."

Recently, I called CiCi's and Sue Tinsley told me that one of the things she remembers Joe saying when he left was, "I made all the money I need right now. It is someone else's turn to make it."

So that you don't think that Joe's thinking is too unusual, let me tell you more about another leader I introduced in an earlier chapter—Pam Nelson, the founder of CCG Systems. She, like Joe, recently sold her company to her employees.

She could have sold it to a large corporation for at least a half million dollars more in personal gain, but decided it was in the best interests of her employees and customers to do an employee stock ownership plan (ESOP). When I asked her why, she said, "What do I need with more money? I have got enough for my family and me now." One of the things Pam had come to grips with was knowing when enough is enough.

> I have always lived conservatively, below my means, so I would have choices. I owned an education company before getting into the technology business with CCG Systems. When I founded CCG in 1987, I did not pay myself for two years. That allowed me to hire more talented people than I otherwise could. A lot of start-ups go through lean times as a matter of course and a lot of good talent gets scared and leaves when you get to the point where you have a tough time making payroll.
>
> Because I had financial flexibility, I could ensure that no one ever missed a paycheck. I know I would have lost some good people who made a great difference in this company if I had to do what many start-ups do, and that is, ask people to accept reduced pay for a while.

A smile of satisfaction came over her face when she said, "One of the great moments of my life was when I handed out the first round of ESOP payout checks to our longer-term employees. Many of those checks were in the hundreds of thousands of dollars. That was a wonderful thing to be able to do!"

Each of the four leaders that I am profiling in this book adhere to similar personal financial principles. This enables them to give large chunks of money away, save for future flexibility, and maintain a current flexibility to make moves they want to make. It has allowed them the exact kind of freedom that Joe Croce spoke about in terms of business risk-taking, and maintaining a high-energy life, unencumbered by the drain of financial stress.

Steve Krajenka was able to make career changes when the opportunities were right and take two years off when he wanted to spend time with his children. Joe Croce is now having a ball with his family. Pam Nelson, while still the key leader at her company, takes weeks off to travel with her partner, parents, and daughters, and has a plan to fully retire in a few years at a young age.

This financial discipline was not a criterion I used to select these leaders. When I decided to write this book in this format, I reviewed the plethora of wonderful leaders I have been privileged to work with through the years and used the criteria in my trust model to select them. I did know early on that I would reference Joe Croce's practice of financial discipline, but didn't realize the parallel with the others until later.

I don't want you to think that I am being idealistic in passing on Joe's wisdom about living on 70 percent of what you make. And frankly, if you can save just 5 percent and even give away 10 percent, you are in a fabulous place in terms of what it will do for you. When my family and I traveled in our motor home for 18 months, I found that this stuff we buy into in the United States where we are slaves to our lifestyles is much easier to break free from than you might think. The truth is that the word *lifestyle* has become a euphemism for greed for many of us.

> **Our contributions should not support our lifestyle.**
> **Our lifestyle should support our contributions.**

Personal financial discipline has allowed these leaders to be trusted at a higher level. They are better able to look out for others because they are not shackled by their personal financial pressures. And ironically, the fact that they kept from being imprisoned by short-term material needs has resulted in their now being able to afford and enjoy substantial material possession.

Financial Goals and Rewards

Joe Croce's personal financial discipline affected his leadership style in some powerful ways. He had the following practice related to setting financial goals at CiCi's, "Their goals were tied to mine. I worked hard to have no hypocrisy. I told people that we were all in this together, and I was careful that my rewards did not over-shadow theirs. There is a peace that comes with that." Joe and his team and their constituents benefited from their united focus on the long term.

You may be thinking that Joe has an advantage because his company is private, and he has more control to be financially disciplined and focused on the long term. There are some publicly traded companies who try to manipulate stock prices by sacrificing long-term financial viability to create short-term rewards. However, these companies are not operating on sound business practices and in many cases are exposing what amounts to a problem with Character Trust. There is an expert in creating shareholder value who makes a solid case that public and private companies should not differ when it comes to financial discipline. Alfred Rappaport is the author of *Creating Shareholder Value: A Guide for Managers and Investors* (New York: Free Press, 1997).

Rappaport wrote an insightful article in the *Harvard Business Review* (September 2006, p. 66) titled: "Ten Ways to Create Shareholder Value." He lays out an important set of recommendations that support the commonsense notion that private and public companies are competing in the same marketplace with the same pool of talent for the same customers and therefore must make the same type of sound compensation, capital, and opportunity investments. He dispels the long-standing myths that justify overpaying corporate chiefs and sacrificing long-term value for short-term gain.

When it comes to the issue of goals and rewards and the subject of trust, there is no denying that many current senior leaders in organizations are hurting and diminishing their ability to lead by having such large gaps between how they get rewarded and how their people are rewarded. This goes to the heart of character trust. Warren Buffett, CEO of Berkshire Hathaway, one of the most successful publicly traded conglomerates, takes a modest salary of $100,000. His other rewards, like Joe's, are tied to the goals of the company. One other thing Joe and Warren have in common is that they like to give money to people who can use some help. Warren—the world's second richest man—gave away 85 percent of his net worth of about 44 billion dollars in 2006.

There are many publicly traded company senior executives who are undermining their employees's trust and their company's success by having large gaps and inconsistencies related to rewards. However, for every one of those, there are many public companies that are doing it right.

Summary of Foundational Character Traits

> *Character may almost be called the most effective means of persuasion.*
>
> —*Aristotle*

By integrating Character Trust into the way you execute and communicate, you create powerful financial and human results. The good news is that any CEO or supervisor can master these competencies. The bad news is that a deficit in one diminishes the rest. Here is a list of traits we proved creates Character Trust:

- Internal honesty (internal reasoning)
- Candor (honesty with others)
- Integrity (doing what you say you will do)
- Humility (internal ability to make others more valuable than yourself)
- Gratitude (actions and words that show humility and the valuing of others)

- Tenacity (deep reserves of energy and commitment)
- Financial discipline (alignment of your values and where you invest money)

There are other character traits that you could certainly add to this list. However, these traits are the minimum required to create and drive execution and communication in a way that generates Radical Trust.

Deficits in any one of these traits will severely weaken your ability to lead if you need talent and are in a competitive environment. There may be some traits you think I forgot to list. However, many character traits we refer to as important for business are actually the result of the successful mastery of combination of the above traits. For example, generosity is the result of humility, gratitude, and financial discipline; and transparency is the result of internal honesty and candor.

> *The whole is more than the sum of the parts.*
> *—Aristotle*

Mastering these foundational traits creates an emotional maturity and stability that is critical to trust. Because of this, deep reservoirs of energy are available to creatively apply to opportunities and challenges.

The word *values* is often used to describe these character traits. For example, you might say: "As a leader, her actions or words are in alignment with her values, therefore, I trust her and enjoy working with her." The way people use the term *values* is synonymous with the character traits we are discussing. So when an employee, customer, or vendor sees a leader that lives his or her values, they are more likely to trust that leader.

We now continue to discuss character, but in the context of skills, strategies, and techniques that build Communication Trust.

PART IV

Communication Trust
(What You Say)

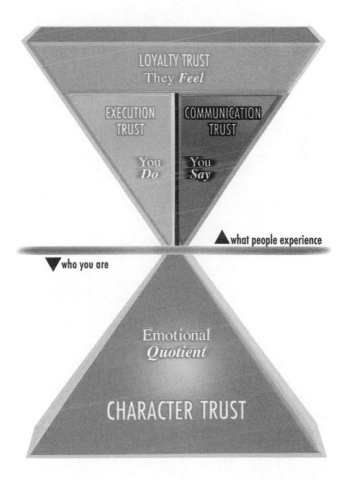

18 | How to Create Cultural Transformation

> *You begin communicating long before you open your mouth.*

I spoke with a manager today of a very large corporation. She told me with frustration that she had just finalized making a lateral move to another part of the corporation to get away from a boss "I just don't trust." He wasn't asking people to do unethical things. In fact, she went on to describe how smart this manager was and how capable in so many ways. However, he had a problem with integrity. She said:

> Other managers are also frustrated. His reputation is taking a hit because the rumor mill is buzzing with stories about politics and conflict that is being blamed on his lack of transparency and directness. People are wasting time figuring out how to cope

135

with this boss instead of spending time on business goals. Others are looking to leave as well.

He would agree on people's roles and then everyone began executing only to bump into each other because he would take authority and decision making away from one person and give it to another in order to "expedite" things. But he would not tell the one whose role or authority was being diminished for the sake of expediency. People felt he lacked courage. To make things worse, when subordinates would try to bring to his attention that he gave conflicting directives, he would sidestep the discussion and try to focus on "bigger" problems in order to avoid owning the mistake.

The group consensus was that his lack of effective communication was generally unintentional, but was viewed as irresponsible. This departing executive said most people felt this boss's haste to make progress drove his credibility-reducing communication mistakes, but this excuse ran thin because of his continued disregard for the consequences. From his perspective, the miscommunications may have seemed to be no big deal. His focus on executing fast was causing him to ignore his relationships with his people. He mistakenly felt that the urgency of the important issues at hand would cause people to overlook or forgive his lack of directness. However, in fact, his low-trust communication was slowing progress.

Most Talented People Leave Low-Trust Bosses

It is important to note that before this problem boss came on the scene, this departing manager was begged to come into her position because of both her knowledge and management skill. She is a major producer in this company and was moved to the corporate headquarters several years earlier because of a successful track record. She has the respect of her subordinates, peers, and senior management. She has received raises and bonuses in the recent past during times when the company was minimizing pay increases due to economic pressure. He is losing a great manager and will have to work harder once she leaves. This is a real example of how what we say as managers impacts our trust and therefore our ability to support speedy execution. Low-trust communication creates an atmosphere of hesitation and even resistance.

Communication Creates Change

The economic reality today is that organizations are making major changes in the way they do business. One way to put it is that we are constantly and radically altering the business models that we follow to do business. This is a good thing. If we fail to adjust, the market place will force us out of business. However, organizations sometimes place all the emphasis on changing processes and systems and often ignore that we also need to transform the way people think and act.

Recently, I was working with a large company who just went through some significant changes related to processes and systems. They anticipated great cost savings and quality improvements; however, they were stalled in the midst of all this change. They were losing good people, quality was suffering, and productivity was way down. One of the executives on the change team that was trying to steer the change expressed frustration that senior management was not dealing with the people side of the business. He said in frustration that these "left-brain leaders thought it all looked good on paper, but they did very little to prepare people for the change." What he is referring to is often called *cultural transformation*.

An example of this is what is happening in the auto industry. Technology, particularly the Internet, has changed the way consumers buy cars. Smart car dealers recognized the shift and began to move away from treating the sale of a car like a negotiated transaction. Instead, smart car dealers changed their focus to become relationship oriented. They realized that if they could change the way they did business and built trust with a customer, they had the opportunity to not only have them come back and buy their next car in a few years, but they could also get the very profitable service business.

Some dealers changed processes and bought new databases that tracked relationship history. They created policies that forced their salespeople to start inputing and tracking data related to the transaction. Some dealers hung big banners on their stores (that was another change, calling themselves "stores") that expressed their desire to "treat you right." But the dealers who did only this kind of process and advertising transformation did not experience much gain.

The dealers who experienced the real gain were those who realized that they had to shift the values and habits of their sales and service people and give them new skills that would enable them to transform from being a salesperson who focused on dogging that transaction until they wore down the consumer to a professional focused on the relationship. Those who successfully made that kind of cultural transformation realized great success. Those who focused solely on processes and rebranding campaigns met with frustration.

Much of this cultural transformation hinges on leaders' ability to communicate. Gaining people's cooperation to change in a big way requires people to be moved both in their head and heart. When a leader communicates from a place of strong character, his or her ability to help people understand and embrace change at a deeper level is more assured.

In fact, the highest accomplishment in communications or leadership is this kind of cultural transformation where you help shift someone's paradigm and value system to a more profitable way of thinking and acting. Take a moment and think of a great manager you have worked for. Then think of the ways they affected your thinking, your outlook or the "ah-hahs" they caused you to have.

Communication is the critical vehicle that allows vision, strategy, and goals to be understood and implemented so progress can be made. In addition, humans are emotional beings. Therefore, communication can inspire, create connections, and drive knowledge sharing. Conversely, poor communication can cause distraction, disconnection, and confusion that adds to the cost of doing business and stifles important shifts from occurring.

High Character Trumps Polish

The best way to improve communication is to improve character.

Managers who learn how to let their character naturally drive their communication find that communication becomes far easier and more successful. You will notice in the upcoming pages a tendency to distill the ideas about Communication Trust into practices that bring forth the strength of your character and challenges you to sharpen your character in additional ways.

You will find this approach refreshing because it allows you to focus on the stuff that makes the most impact and does not waste time at the surface with techniques that are often awkward. I provide practical tips that will make it easier for you to practice these skills or teach others to apply them in their daily routines.

Character's Role in Communication

You might say people's perception of our character is driven by how we live our values. People with strong character keep their values at the top of their mind so it shapes what they say and do. The same awareness of values that shapes our actions, should shape our communication.

Another way of saying it is that what we say is naturally and easily molded and expressed based on our internal values or lack of values. So people with underdeveloped character must work much harder and expend much more energy to communicate effectively.

People who take time to live their values are also creating a foundation from which effective communication springs.

Character Traits That Support Communication Trust

There is an old saying that relates to communication: "It is not *what* you say, it is *how* you say it." Often the tone of voice and body language you use are more powerful than the words you use. Communication is not like an onion with multiple layers. It is like an apple. The firm, smooth texture of the skin is supported by the fruit underneath. And just as the firmness of the fruit provides the structure for the look and feel, character supports both what you say and how you say it (especially body language and tone).

In fact, I challenge you to monitor the communication of a manager you know who has strong character. You will see that the manager's messages are delivered with more impact. You might analyze that it is because of his or her body language and tone. However, that manager is not consciously driving body language and tone so much as his or her character is automatically driving them. People interpret what you mean based on who you are (your character) which is often translated through body language and tone of voice.

> ***What you say is greatly affected by how you say it, but meaning is derived from the listener's trust in who you are.***

That's why people tend to do business with those whom they have a relationship. The relationship tells them who you are and sets the context for everything else. Now remember, we are talking about talented people here. Yes, some people can fool a lot of people into thinking they are trustworthy when in truth they have little character. Politicians are not the only ones who try to appear to have character because it sells. However, we are not talking about manipulating the masses. In this book, we are talking about people in business that you want to partner with to achieve results and with whom you interact regularly.

Communication Skills of a High-Trust Manager

In the next four chapters, I will show you how to integrate your character with the four most important communication skills and achieve the kind of excellence in communication that can yield cultural transformation. You may also want to use these to coach your people. Chances are you have witnessed people engaged in negative conflict because one of these four is not being integrated into the way they communicate.

There are four fundamental things that impact the level of trust someone gives your communication: *Credibility, Clarity, Sensitivity,* and *Brevity.* If character is developed and used to drive how you communicate related to each one of these, communication is much easier and more successful.

19

Credibility Leads to Cooperation and Buy-In

One of the critical bottlenecks in performance stems from the fact that many managers are only partially believable. If a manager is not totally trusted in what he says, people act on what he says with more caution. The boss in Chapter 18 who is causing his manager to change departments is not believable and therefore is distracting people and slowing people down as well as losing talent.

There are many traits and skills that a manager must master to be believable. The payoff is significant. If you show me a great leader, I will show you someone who worked at developing the things I talk about in this chapter related to credibility. Let's pick up our discussion of a critical character trait that is fundamental to communication—humility.

Leaders with Humility Are a Magnet and Catalyst for Talent

In 1990, I started to note the traits of leaders I had worked with that enabled them to be exceptional leaders. Humility was one of the common traits I identified. I was curious to see if great leaders from history would reflect this. The problem is that the big thing that separates business leaders of the past 50 years from leaders prior to that, is that there was not nearly as much competitive pressure. So I wanted to find an area where I could study leaders from the past that were in competitive arenas.

Business prior to the 1960s hinged largely on the capital you had access to and not your ability to compete or lead others to compete. But I discovered that one area that has been highly competitive for a couple centuries was the pursuit of the U.S. presidency. Granted, there are many times beyond recent history where the best candidates were not running, but there are many occasions in U.S. history where some very competent and capable leaders competed for the White House.

I began studying U.S. presidents. Interestingly, humility showed up as an indicator of success. Washington clearly had it. Adams beat the supposed genius, Jefferson, to the White House partially because of it. Lincoln is revered for it. David McCullough's Pulitzer Prize winning book, *Truman* (New York: Simon & Schuster, 1993) reveals that congressmen from both parties claimed they trusted the humble Truman more than any other president they served under. Eisenhower was promoted over many generals who were previously senior to him, including Generals Patton and MacArthur, because of his leadership abilities. You may recall that both of these generals had sizable egos. Once again, the leader who had more humility was entrusted with the greater leadership roles during the war and after.

Then I came across an article in the *Harvard Business Review* by Jim Collins that was written years before his best-selling book,

Good to Great. His research revealed that great leaders possessed two critical traits: tenacity and humility. So let me underscore the validity of this character trait that is critical to credibility and thus Communication Trust.

Just like I did with the other competencies, I will use a leader to demonstrate how mastery of this competency impacts others. The leader I want to use in this case is Harry, and I will step beyond Harry to share with you the level of talent that Harry drew and retains at his organization. This story reveals how Harry's humility attracted a very talented leader YES needed who was also a prominent attorney and judge—Rufus Banks. It is important to note that Harry's organization is grassroots and does not have the glamor, notoriety, or money that often draws high-talent leaders. This organization is a roll-up-your-sleeves organization that doesn't pay its board members and key committee chairs.

Power of Humility

It was a frigid February evening in 1999. Rufus Banks and his wife, Shavaughn, had just returned from visiting Shavaughn's family. He had a bad cold and went right to bed. Just as Rufus was getting comfortable under the covers, Shavaughn answered the phone. It was Ken Melvin, a Virginia state senator and criminal defense attorney whom Rufus had battled many times in court when he was a state prosecutor.

Rufus had not spoken to Ken in a while, and his initial thought was that Ken was calling about a campaign contribution. Little did he know that this call would change his life. Because he felt so ill, Rufus was not excited about taking a fund-raising call even if it was from the Senator himself. Rufus, like Harry, is very willing to inconvenience himself for his family, colleagues, clients, and friends. This is a specific trait of humble people; they don't put themselves ahead of others. Current-day thinking teaches that you won't get ahead if you don't toot your own horn or make yourself number one. This story disproves that popular notion as misguided pop-psychology.

In spite of his ailment and the assumption that the call was a fund-raising call, Rufus took the call. To his surprise, it was not about a campaign contribution. It was a much bigger request that would uproot him from his current, very successful role in private practice with one of the most distinguished law firms in Virginia.

Ken told Rufus that there was wide support in the House of Delegates to make him a judge and there was an opening in juvenile court that they wanted to consider him for. Rufus's confirmation was one of the quickest in state history and no doubt it had a lot to do with his humility and credibility.

Rufus is a high-talent professional who has very little time to do volunteer work, but a juvenile judge would add tremendous expertise to the YES organization. Rufus joined the YES Board. When I interviewed Rufus, the first question I asked him was what drew him to YES. He said, "It was the work YES was doing and Harry's humility and lack of selfish ambition."

It is important to note that even though Harry does not have the luxury of using money to attract and motivate talent, his ability to engage and inspire talent as a result of his credibility is directly applicable to a for-profit environment.

I want to define more fully what humility means in a business sense. Wikipedia (www.wikipedia.com) offers some sound insight about people and concepts, and their reference to humility adds to our discussion: "A humble person is generally thought to be unpretentious and modest: someone who does not think that he or she is better or more important than others."

Let me put this in a business context. Managers who lack humility create distractions to business goals and outcomes because of their personal and political agendas. Conversely, managers who practice humility permit greater openness and vulnerability, which is critical to an environment where people's talent is maximized.

> *Arrogance conveys: "I am to be valued."*
> *Humility conveys: "You are to be valued."*

Ambition's Role in Leadership

Here is a common source of a lack of humility: ambition. So often we encounter bosses who take credit for a subordinate's ideas or bosses who make decisions that clearly benefit their careers while ignoring the careers of others. It is rather telling that describing someone as ambitious has to be put into context before you know if it is derogatory or complimentary. Is it solely self-focused or is it balanced so that his or her ambition extends to other's careers and needs?

> *Too much personal ambition slows things down.*

Consider Edward T. Davis. He is known as Big Ed around YES. His six-foot frame projects strength and his face projects thoughtfulness. Ed is a reserved young man of few words, but a guy you would want holding down the fort. He was destined to fall through the cracks. Like so many at-risk youth, he did not find his confidence in sports or formal academics. There aren't many options for building esteem in the inner city. Ed is smart and a genius with computers. In his environment growing up, there was very little to encourage his development. Ed was one of many kids whose great potential was being overlooked until Harry showed up.

Ed summarized his first encounter with YES as "suspicious." He did not believe it was "for real." He had seen many not-so-well-intended men pretending to care, "but only using the kids to get what they wanted." He remembers seeing all the equipment in one of the YES studios and his response was that "something was off." Ed reminds me of many corporate citizens who have become jaded and suspicious of management. In fact, employees of the other leaders I am using as case studies told me the same thing. At first, they could not believe these people were "for real." But when they found out that their ambition was not singularly focused on their own success, but the company's success, they were, as one person put it, "thrilled."

Ed said that as he got to know Harry, his mind changed. "Harry came in here and told us the vision. What got me is that he used to show up and talk one-on-one to us. I told Harry I was good with computers. And he actually trusted me and put me to work helping with YES's computers." This is indicative of what today's leaders do so well. You may recall that Steve did this: Identified talent and engaged it. Ed stated, "My suspicion didn't go away immediately. But I kept seeing Harry helping kids . . . and over time I realized that he is very genuine."

By Ed's own admission, he was not an easy sell. Like so many employees, Ed did not know what he needed. But Harry helped to get him in the right seat. And in spite of Ed's reluctance to buy in, he did. Ed went through most of the training programs YES offered. He learned marketable skills. More importantly, the curriculum taught him how to build and be on a team and lead. He went through activities and training that forced young people to take on the roles of artist and producer and form teams that would actually create, record, produce, and market music CDs in their neighborhoods.

In spite of a childhood full of broken trust, Ed staked his future on Harry's credibility. It was not easy. He did not live close to one of the studios. He had to do a lot of walking and bus riding. It was also hard work. Like many people with computer skills, Ed became a go-to guy. He never turned other young people away.

Where Ed went from here is a testament to the power of a partnership. Ed describes it this way: "I was a senior in high school and Ms. Danene (executive director of YES) and Harry asked me if I wanted to go to school. I had very bad grades. But they saw my talent with computers and knew that I was a lot smarter than my grades showed. They told me I should go to college. Just Harry telling me I should go to college gave me faith in myself and made me take it seriously."

This is an extremely valuable trait of Radical Trust leaders. They help people find, believe and then hone their talents. This is the real kind of nonfluff motivation that Radical Trust provides.

Danene lobbied the president of Livingstone College, Dr. Algeania Freeman, who had long been recruiting her. Instead of getting a great communications professor, the president got a great student and gave him a full scholarship. Ed is now a senior with a 3.0 grade-point-average. When he is home on break, he can be found behind a computer or mixing board at one of the studios helping other young people.

Ed is proof that people who are in need, often trust, respond to, and follow people who have the right kind of ambition. To many, it is a surprise that the helping hand YES is trying to extend is viewed by at-risk youth with suspicion and mistrust, but this is no different than the similar struggle so many organizations have in engaging their people. However, once trust is established, things can and do change.

Take Responsibility, but Give Others the Credit

Many leaders follow the adage that: "I take responsibility for problems and mistakes, but I never take credit for success. Instead, I pass it to my team." Many people fail to recognize that ultimately leaders don't need credit for individual projects or accomplishments. A leader's ability is best expressed by the numerous successes of his teams. Passing credit on is not as self-sacrificing as it appears. It is simply good for everyone. A leader's success is measured by what his or her people produce.

Before Harry left his career in television to found YES, he was the senior vice president of family productions and vice president of original programming with the Family Channel. In television, networks produce many original programs. The hit show, *Friends,* is an example of original programming that NBC created in concert with a third-party production company.

In Hollywood, people grow their careers based on the productions they have credits for. That is why shows are careful to give credit to so many. Ambition can become a problem when some executives who are politically powerful demand credits even though they don't contribute to the project.

When Harry first arrived at the Family Channel, he found there was friction over senior executives getting credit on projects where they made little or no contribution. Harry felt this was causing resentments that reduced creativity and collaboration. He made a tough decision that mandated that no one would be listed in credits unless they directly contributed to the project. Initially when he made the decision, some felt he took unnecessary political risk. His boss was one of the biggest abusers of credits.

Harry's subordinates were relieved and saw the wisdom in the decision because they were now free from the distraction this was causing. Harry's boss was irritated with Harry in the short-run, but he too came around when he found out that Harry refused to be listed in any credits.

Ironically, I think this kind of display of guts and credibility drew the former head of NBC, Brandon Tartikoff, to join YES's board.

Listening Is Not the Problem

Our own needs can scream so loudly, that we don't hear others.

Show me a manager who is a poor listener and I will show you a person who probably is too tuned in to his or her own needs. People waste a lot of time on listening skills that focus on creating (or manipulating) the perception that you listen. The real result that talented people want is not your fake attention, but your genuine concern and understanding.

Let me approach this from a very practical level. The kind of creativity and innovation we need from talented people today requires them to think and communicate about complex issues. If we as leaders fail to plug into and hear our people effectively, they will quickly tire of having to work extra hard to compensate for our inability to get it. And if we don't understand our people's needs at a deep level, we cannot be advocates for them and their talent.

I have had the good fortune to coach some extremely talented leaders who are being stunted by deficits in some of the traits we discussed related to the competency of Character Trust. As they make progress with humility and ambition, I almost always get feedback that they are also becoming better listeners or are more astute, yet we spent no time on traditional skills related to listening.

If you or one of your managers has been accused of poor listening, you will find that these principles about humility and ambition may point to the real root problem. All of these leaders would tell you as I would, that we all at one point or another struggle with our personal ambition and humility.

> *Humility is a doorway to opportunity, but requires constant diligence to keep it open.*

Candor—Not an Option—A Necessity

When I referenced internal honesty and integrity earlier, I told you we would come back to this issue that speaks to our ability to be honest with others in a way that is beneficial. It was very evident that a great deal of Steve's execution success stems from his candor. But the big questions are: Why aren't more managers like the ones in this book? Why is it so common for managers to struggle with candor? One reason is because many managers have not learned how effective candor really is. I know this sounds simple. But it is true. Candor requires that you be willing to risk some short-term discomfort in exchange for long-term gain, and we live in a world that is shortsighted and likes to avoid discomfort. So avoidance is a common practice in life and in management.

In fact, the outcome of applying the four communication skills in this competency results in much higher levels of candor. In the next chapters on clarity, brevity, and sensitivity, I provide a host of tips and techniques that help managers to increase their candor.

You may relate to the list that follows because you or someone you lead needs to recognize what may be holding them back from being more candid:

- Some managers are just so busy they don't realize that being more candid would help them be more productive. I demonstrated this in Execution Trust when I revealed that Steve saves a ton of time for himself and his people because he is so candid.

- Some managers are just not assertive enough. These next three chapters will help tremendously if you or someone you know needs to learn to communicate more assertively.

- Some managers are beyond candid and are what I call dysfunctionally blunt. What I mean is that they use their insight and judgment to beat people down rather than lift them up. Again, these four chapters on Communication Trust challenge this kind of manager to shift their paradigm and give specific and practical tips to channel their insight and ideas so as to be productively candid. The fundamental difference between being dysfunctionally blunt and productively candid is that when you and the other person move beyond the dialogue, they experience both clarity about what to do and they are more motivated and confident about doing it.

- And let's be frank: There are managers who have used manipulation to advance their careers so much so that it has been habit forming. However, even though the mistakes these people make tend to generate a lot of pain and noise, they are in the minority.

The example I used in an earlier chapter of the CEO from American Airlines being less than candid with his employees was a strategy to deal with a business problem. His strategy failed and he learned a painful lesson. American Airlines's culture also gained a valuable lesson about candor. They all witnessed the consequence of his actions. The board asked him to leave. American Airlines's success in maintenance is a direct result of the elevated state of candor that followed.

It may sound odd, but candor is a learned behavior. As Enron and so many other scandals proved, this habit of candor can be unlearned as well. One of the greatest influences a leader can have on a corporate culture is setting the pace for how candid people become. I say this to emphasize your role as a leader. If you are a senior leader, you shave an enormous responsibility. Your candor will ripple out in the organization and inspire others to higher levels of candor. Or your lack of candor will move like a wall of waves, creating instability and uncertainty about taking the risk to be candid.

You may be in middle management or a supervisor and have the misfortune to be in a culture where tradition and/or senior leaders have influenced the current climate with a less than candid culture. This means that you will have to work harder to be candid. But please remember, having bosses who are less than genuine is no excuse for you to be less than genuine. Our people still deserve our candor regardless of whether we get if from our boss. Life is not fair. This is one of the reasons leadership can be lonely.

Let me give you an example of just how contagious candor can be.

The Secret to a Leader's Use of Candor

The reason Pam Nelson is able to be so productively candid is she has developed the complementary character traits that are necessary for productive candor: humility, valuing of others, and internal honesty. Consider this statement by a client of CCG Systems, Marilyn L. Rawlings, fleet manager, Lee County, Florida:

> Pam has the ability to make you feel that you are the center of her universe for the time you are together. Whether you are in a meeting or just having dinner, she listens intently and purposefully. She may have other things on her mind, but you would never know it. She is focused and involved in every word you speak. Because you know she is really listening rather than "giving face time," you listen in return when she "speaks the truth in love" back to you. She will not be telling you what you *want to hear,* but what you *need to hear.* As a leader, it is often difficult to hear the truth. Because I trust Pam, I know the truth coming from her is not spoken to hurt me but to help me. She is a great accountability partner.

Humility creates the opportunity to invest in others and leads directly to the trait of valuing others. As I said before, you can be humble and still not value other people. There are many religious people who are humble relative to seeing themselves as less than God. However, some of these same people can show no mercy to others because their own interests are so consuming. Strangely, that very devaluing of others, puts them in contradiction to the teaching of the God they claim to serve who calls them to love others as themselves. I am not knocking faith here. But many religions, including mine, are like many corporations. They need to develop a fuller range of character traits.

Pam weaves together her humility with a deep sense of value for others and then couples that with candor. Pam takes liberty to challenge people in a professional and loving way at a character level. As a result of being exposed to this level of candor, many at CCG Systems have begun working on their character at a deeper level.

Let me stop for a moment because you may think it odd that I used the word *love* in relation to managing people in the workplace, and I don't want you to think I am being idealistic. The other occasion in this book that the word love was used was by a hard-charging, tough president of a 600-store franchise that is in a brutally competitive business. That was Craig Moore, the current president of CiCi's Pizza. In Chapter Two, he described Joe Croce and his application of tough love. And that is what I am getting at with Pam. The more productive the relationship is, the more candor there is. Nothing expresses love more than caring enough to tell the truth even though there is risk.

Pam and these other leaders work to maintain a strength of character so that it becomes natural for them to execute and express at a more productive level, and it draws everyone to a better place. This leads me to the most important message of this book:

Critical leadership traits (like candor) are only mastered effectively when we have the right combination of character traits operating in unison. Leadership traits that seem unattainable only appear that way because we have failed to recognize and develop specific character traits.

One of the strategic reasons candor is so critical to business success in competitive times is that creativity depends on it. Creativity is simply recognizing a truth that other people don't yet see and exploiting it before competitors do. So, if you as a manager foster an environment that embraces candor over comfort or short-term gain, you do a great deal to promote innovation. The biggest difference between an innovative culture and one that isn't is the level of candor.

This subject of credibility requires that we focus on "who you are" so "what you say" is credible. Therefore, this chapter has given you insights about traits and values that shape the way you think about communication (your paradigm). To round out our discussion of credibility, here are the most common excuses that managers give for diminished candor:

Excuse for Lack of Candor	*Reality*
1. It helps morale. The truth will scare them.	It may not make them happy in the short-term, but it will definitely hurt morale in the long-run.
2. It's just easier.	It isn't. It just appears that way. Avoiding conflict only makes things fester.
3. They don't need to know. It is private or information that must be kept confidential.	That's fine, but don't avoid the subject. If they ask, be frank. Tell them that it is a discussion you must keep private or confidential, but be polite about it.

Excuse for Lack of Candor	*Reality*
4. I don't have time to get into the details.	So tell them, but be polite.
5. It will make me look weak if they know the truth. Particularly when it is my mistake.	You will look weaker when they find out.
6. I had to give a quick response. I didn't have time to think.	That's not the only quick response. There is nothing wrong with delay. "Let me think about that and get back to you" is often very acceptable. Or simply pausing during an uncomfortable situation until you are more comfortable with your response is always an option.
7. My emotions got the best of me.	Some of the best leaders I know are very passionate and emotional, but they have learned that as soon as negative emotions surface or conflict gets heated, they slow way down to avoid saying something they regret.
8. The truth may hurt someone.	Nothing hurts a relationship more than a lack of candor.

20 | Clarity Leads to Engagement

I want to share what another high-talent individual learned from a Radical Trust leader about achieving clarity in communication. Adam McFaddin Ballard is a young man who was featured in Dan Rather's book, *The American Dream* (New York: Harper Paperbacks, 2002). Dan Rather profiled Adam's life because he grew up in the tough streets of Compton, California then went on to live his dream of becoming a filmmaker.

In 1995, when Adam was 15 he attended a three-week YES media summer camp. In 1996, he returned to YES's summer camp on production and film making. During the next summer at the film camp, Adam was chosen to be the director for a public service announcement for Boys & Girls Clubs of America.

YES has been somewhat self-sustaining as a result of some of the commercials they produce. Seeing Adam's commercial in 2000 was one of the things that grabbed my family's heart and pushed us toward a decision to join YES. If you visit the YES web site (www.YesAmerica.org), you can see that commercial.

Adam identified a communication trait that Harry uses in the very competitive and complex business of film making to create clarity: context.

The Power of Context

Adam was the assistant director for the production of a music video for Maverick Records, the label for Madonna and the Deftones. Because of a crisis, he was suddenly thrust into the role of director. The morning of the shoot, the crew began asking Adam why the director was not on the set. Adam had no answer until an hour before shooting was to start and the producer called him to reveal that the director's car had careened off the road on the way to work and flipped over an embankment.

Adam would have to be the acting director that day. He navigated a complex morning successfully. Later the injured director made it to the location to lend a hand. Adam's challenge became more complex when the drugs the hospital gave the director made him groggy, causing him to fall asleep frequently during the shoot. So the director could not direct; he could only second guess Adam's ability by periodically providing advice between naps. This created Adam's real challenge by adding another level of confusion since it was unclear if Adam was director or if the director was still directing.

Stress Minimizes Talent—Focus Harnesses It

Adam said he remembered how Harry would keep people focused by setting context, and he set about doing the same. What Adam meant by context was that he made sure he had clarity with everyone about the objectives of the shoot. He reviewed any out-of-the-ordinary aspect of the scene they were going to shoot before they proceeded. He checked with the crew frequently to see that they were all on the same page. The thing Adam had noticed about Harry is that any time there was complexity or stress, Harry would take a moment to have a conversation to ensure he had clarity on any aspect of the work that was out of the ordinary. When Harry did this, he created placeholders in people's minds that referenced a critical concept or need so that when it came time to execute, they had quick recall on what was needed for that specific item.

This may sound simple, but given time pressures, there is often the belief that there is not time for this kind of checking. This is similar to a point many of my clients say they got from Rudolph W. Giuliani's book, *Leadership* (New York: Hyperion, 2002). He references the value of regular well-run meetings where there is meaningful dialogue. Many cultures have gotten so dysfunctional about meetings that they avoid them as if the meetings are the problem. One of the things Giuliani's book did was to make meetings or dialogue a part of doing business rather than a distraction from it. The kind of discourse that took place at Giuliani's regular meetings is what Adam was doing in his meeting.

Adam learned from Harry to identify the key issues that set the context for what is important in the work that was about to be done. This focused talented people's energy on the right things. Adam commented that in some work the need to have focusing conversations with greater frequency is the key to true collaboration and productivity. Adam's crew, like a lot of people, didn't like formal meetings. But the fact that the crew could expect that before each major step there would be an opportunity to focus and adjust made everyone relax and execute.

Many leaders today feel they have to be overly participative and democratic and so they bog down communication with too much give and take. One thing that helped Adam on this particular day was remembering how Harry was not afraid to take the reins and dictate what needed to be done. Harry's high level of humility and respect for people gave him wide latitude to dictate what needed to be done without the consequence of resentment.

Adam learned from Harry that increasing the frequency of dialogue when things are complex and confusing is important and that being directive can be a necessary part of leadership. The right frequency of dialogue can give a leader permission to be situational in his style of leadership and move from participative to directive when necessary.

Adam is currently an independent filmmaker, writer, and director. He graduated from the prestigious Art Center College of Design in Pasadena, California where he now resides. Adam still comes to YES's headquarters to give his time to produce various projects. Adam is working with YES to produce a public service announcement for Virginia's Alcohol Beverage Control Board.

The Power of Attitude in Communication

If we, as managers, are going to be clear about what we say, we must address an important issue. People interpret what you communicate based on subconscious influences. One of many fields of study that focuses on this is neural linguistic programming (NLP). Even though it can be very beneficial to learn more about how the brain processes information, you can master a principle that is critical for managers to understand without an in-depth knowledge of the science behind it. This critical principle is how a manager's mood affects the clarity of his messages.

Resetting Your Attitude

Since I have been involved with YES and Harry, I have seen Harry move from one highly stressful situation to another without tainting the next conversation with backwash from the previous one.

I have noticed that he goes through a mental break when he goes from one situation or person to the next. In studying this closely, it actually appears that he is resetting his mind. In the same way rebooting a computer erases the temporary memory and "refreshes" it for other uses, Harry seems to be able to erase negative emotions and keep them from diminishing his next encounter.

The result of this is that Harry is perceived as a very consistent person who does not let emotion dictate his style of leading or communicating.

Power of a Consistent Attitude

I find that our culture accepts that it is okay to be moody. In fact, there are personality profiles that are used to incorrectly teach that if you are a driver type leader, it is okay to be pushy, argumentative, and moody. Of course, this is more a sign of immaturity than it is of a style of leadership. Nonetheless, there is large acceptance of managers acting poorly because they're having a bad day.

Here are a couple techniques I've seen Harry and many other leaders use to reset their circuitry to shed stress and bring clarity through consistent energy and focus to the next conversation. I refer to this as PEP:

- *Pause:* Before engaging in the next conversation, pause. One way to do this is to take care of noting any to-dos or information from the last conversation before you go to the next. This action often allows you to channel the stress of the last exchange into perspective.
- *Engage:* Create, review, or voice the purpose, agenda, and time limit for the next discourse.

■ *Precall:* Address the stress that you are bringing with you if you are having a hard time shaking it. I have seen Harry and other leaders do this, but infrequently. At the beginning of the conversation, they address what could be misperceived. For example, I've heard Harry say, "Forgive me, I just finished a very demanding conversation. If I seem stressed, it has nothing to do with this conversation."

Also, being consistent to achieve greater clarity does not mean that we become stoic or void of emotion. In fact, there will be times that you as a leader need to convey frustration and disappointment. The key is that you are maturely choosing to express those emotions in a professional way. Here is an important tip: On occasion it is okay to express frustration or disappointment in a problem in front of a group. However, if the frustration or disappointment is directed at an individual, it is almost always important to do that in private with that person. Harry consciously uses emotion to make a point. Less able managers let emotion blindly drive the message.

Pace

If you talk too fast, people can become skeptical or just not keep up with you. Some people subconsciously get their guard up when people talk fast. Speaking in a long-winded or slow voice also affects clarity.

But let's go beyond the simple need to speak at the right pace. Let me ask you a question: Do you, as a manager, move at a fast pace through your day? If you answered "yes," here is an important question: How approachable do your people perceive you to be? If your people feel they can approach you to gain clarity about issues, you are in a good place. However, if you are like many managers, people may be reluctant to approach you to gain clarity because you are so busy—always in a hurry. Are you frequently talking fast and dashing on? This could be dangerous. Many people are willing to stay in a state of low clarity rather than approach a manager who seems to be in a hurry, and that slows down execution or productivity. Many years ago, I learned a painful lesson about how our pace translates into a perception about our leadership that can cause employees to minimize communication with us.

Lack of Clarity Is Expensive

Back in the late 1980s, I left corporate banking to run a start-up company. I was an investor and the managing partner. We had just opened our fourth store two days prior. By this point in the evolution of the company, we had a solid management team in place. We had been having team meetings that helped us keep the opening of this fourth store on track. In fact, because of the additional team dialogue, this store's opening was the most successful of all our stores. We felt that this location was going to be great, and we were right.

Several weeks prior to opening this store, we were trying to decide whether to delay the grand opening. Often in retail, a store is opened and time is taken to get all the processes and systems running properly before doing all the grand opening advertising to drive volume. That is why you sometimes see a grand opening weeks after a store actually opens.

In our case, since we were a small start-up, the practice was to do the grand opening at the same time that the store actually opened because cash flow was critical. Therefore, everyone assumed that we would do what we had previously done, and that was to do all the grand opening advertising to drive volume at the same time as we opened the store.

I remember that a small voice in my head made me pause out of fear that if we drive too much volume with the normal discounting, we could hurt sales by creating quality problems. But that quiet voice in my head was overwhelmed by a much louder voice I frequently heard. And that was the voice of *CASH FLOW* which regularly stressed me out.

Growing a business organically put a lot of demand on the need for cash. So I proceeded with doing the grand opening the week the store opened. It overwhelmed our capacity.

It was around midnight at our main office and most of the management team was working late trying to keep up with the volume our advertising had driven to this great location. My key manager, Tracy, was zooming past me in the hall as I acknowledged our dilemma by saying: "Who would have thought something so good could go so bad?" Later our financials showed that because we overdrove volume, we created quality problems and lost customers. We lost around $100,000 in revenue that year. For a business our size, that was a huge mistake.

Upon hearing my words, Tracy in her typical candor said, "Yeah, I thought this was going to happen." I was shocked and stopped dead in my tracks and spun around and snapped back, "Did you say you thought this would happen?" She interrupted her stride with a pause and then turned because she could hear the pain in my voice. She said, "Yes, Joe. I thought if we did the grand opening at the beginning before we got a handle on this store, we would be blown out of the water."

I trusted Tracy's judgment. And if she had voiced her concern, that would have pushed me over the edge to hold off on the advertising discounts that overdrove volume. So I said, "Tracy, why didn't you tell me this sooner?"

She was tired so she fumbled through a couple excuses like, "You are Mr. Strategic Planner . . . and I thought you had a handle on that. . . . And besides you have more experience at this than I do." But she stopped and had this look on her face that expressed she was thinking something and didn't want to say it. Then she blurted, "Joe, I thought you knew what you were talking about."

When I told my wife what happened, she pegged it when she said, "Joe, you are moving too fast. Your employees all think that you are in such a hurry taking care of business that they have to have something really urgent before they approach you." My pace was sending a message that a lack of clarity about why we were doing what we were doing was okay, because Joe is in control.

Having Tracy share her concern about the situation would have made me reconsider this critical decision. Tracy and I took some time to undo what remained of her perception that "I knew what I was talking about." She then began to take more initiative for shaping and voicing strategy for our business.

> *Your actions scream so loudly that*
> *I can't hear what you are saying!*

Your pace sends a loud message to people about your approachability. There is nothing inherently wrong with being in a hurry, but leaders must be aware that a fast pace can equate to people minimizing their communication. And it can devalue people and affect their morale. Have you heard the adage about change: You can't over-communicate during a time of change. Let me add to that:

> *During change, it is a leader's job to be sure*
> *that the fast pace doesn't compromise clarity.*

21

Sensitivity Leads to Accountability

There is a business concept called the *Balanced Scorecard* that was coined in the book by the same name written by Robert S. Kaplan and David Norton (Boston: Harvard Business School Press, 1996). This book makes the case that businesses cannot afford to focus on only one group of constituents like shareholders or customers and be profitable for the long haul. The premise of this widely embraced concept is that the leaders of the organization must be sensitive to the various constituent groups that impact profitability which include customers, shareholders, employees, vendors, communities, and others.

Communication Trust is critical to success with a balanced scorecard. In the past, managers reserved their best communication for those who meant the most to the organization. That translated to mean that managers communicated with great sensitivity to their bosses up the chain and to the customers. But when it came to vendors or employees who may be considered less important, there was a different level of sensitivity or respect. You might say the level of respect demonstrated in the communication was situational, depending on with whom the manager was communicating.

If you study great leaders, one thing people often say of them is that they treat everyone the same—with the same amount of deference or respect. I am using the word sensitivity and respect to mean that we show people we value them. Since we live in more of a balanced scorecard world today, managers are now accountable to make people feel valued regardless of where they are in the pecking order or food chain.

The Power of Respect

> *People don't care how much you know until they know how much you care.*

Let me take you back to Harry's office at the YES pilot studio. On this particular day, Harry was dealing with a series of very stressful and even volatile situations at his office.

Several visitors dropped into the pilot studio unannounced. Do you remember the movie *Stand by Me* about a principal who used unorthodox methods to turn the school around? Officials from the school that the movie was based on were in the area for an education conference and heard about YES and decided to drop in and check it out. Harry's reaction to and treatment of these people makes a powerful point of how Radical Trust leaders connect with others and use warmth and respect to make them feel valued.

Knowing how much stress Harry was under, I was again fascinated to watch him reset his brain to leave the stress behind and greet each one of these people with warmth and engagement. Each person felt Harry was fully present and would have never guessed that they had interrupted several important discussions. All they knew was that they were important to him. The fascinating thing is that with this value established, he was able to expedite this meeting and hand these people off to someone else for a tour. The way you greet people is powerful in establishing the kind of rapport that causes someone to begin to give you trust. After returning to New Jersey, these visitors initiated the establishment of a YES studio at their high school and the proceeds YES received for its work paid for 10 at-risk teenage girls to participate in a 10-week communication program.

You Don't Have to Like People to Value Them

You may think that this is easy for Harry because he naturally has a heart for people. That is what I thought. However, I nearly fell off my chair when Harry told me one day "I don't like people much."

Because of all he had seen, he had become jaded by the fact that most of us go on enjoying life while so many kids live in pain and suffering. In addition, he is a creative introvert and enjoys being by himself. I am telling you this because I want you to understand that Communication Trust does not depend on personality or communications style. It is really about character. It is false to assume that gregarious or extroverted people are inherently better equipped to build Radical Trust.

Feedback Is Not Optional

Because this chapter is emphasizing sensitivity, it is important to note that the use of that word does not mean that because someone will be put off or uncomfortable with feedback, it should be avoided. Sensitivity is third in this series of four communication skills because credibility and clarity are more important.

> *A manager's lack of assertiveness is often the result of making sensitivity more important than credibility and clarity.*

There is a reference from the 27th chapter of Proverbs in the *Bible* that sheds light on the issue of feedback: "the wounds from a friend can be trusted, but an enemy multiplies kisses." In this age, trusted leaders need to recognize that the risk of injury should not dissuade us from feedback. If we as a leader have the right kind of relationship with our people we are much better equipped to "sensibly" approach the person with feedback that is productive.

Leaders like Harry do the hard work to earn your trust through a relationship so he can risk wounding you with a truth you need to hear. The verse right before it, says: "Better is open rebuke than hidden love." A lot of leaders let us down because while they may care about us deeply, if they don't invest in the business of on-going candid feedback, we are often denied valuable opportunities to grow.

Because Harry forces himself to value people and earnestly shows it, he has the kind of permission that managers, salespeople, and parents would find more valuable than gold. Harry has permission to be absolutely candid with people. One of the great benefits of trust from a communication standpoint is that once established, people open up more or let down their guard.

Vulnerability Is Not Always a Sign of Weakness

When we choose to be vulnerable with talented people, they often then have a greater willingness to reveal to us new insights and information. All of these great leaders are willing to receive feedback from their talented subordinates. And their vulnerability is a powerful example. It, in fact, inspires confidence among most people. Don't get me wrong; if you don't trust someone, you are not setting a good example by pretending to be open to their insights when in fact you shouldn't be.

Previous chapters have proven that each of these leaders demonstrates a level of sensitivity and accountability in the way they communicate because of their mastery of character. Although, the tips in this chapter may be helpful, the real traits that lead to sensitivity and accountability were laid out earlier in this book.

22 | Brevity Leads to Influence

> **People are more willing to listen to people who are good at getting to the point.**

There is a word that embodies the ability to be brief but thorough in communicating. That word is *direct*. Being direct and to the point is a common trait of great leaders. Transparency unlocks the ability to be direct.

Transparency: The Key to Brevity

> **Transparency simplifies communication.**

Transparency is a great word because it infers that our communication should be void of hidden agendas and that our motivation should be as clear as glass. Here is a good example of transparency from another great leader.

Mother Teresa died with seven possessions. Therefore, you cannot second-guess her motivation as to why she was serving the needy in India. It is not like she had a clothing line she was simultaneously pushing. She is a great example because she shows the power of transparency to focus people on the right things.

She was a tough and savvy leader who achieved a great deal of practical benefit for thousands of people. And here is the kicker: Over 10,000 people took a vow of chastity and poverty to follow her. I mean you talk about sober realities. I doubt many of us could get our people to set or achieve those kinds of goals.

Transparency is the result of mastering internal honesty and candor at a high level. Here are some tips that will help.

Eliminate Communication Distractions

> *We communicate to express not to impress.*
> —*Winston Churchill*

Since Joe Croce sold CiCi's Pizza, he has attended many investment meetings in New York's financial community, and he shared an interesting observation about the cost of a lack of transparency: "I was sitting through a pitch to a group of investors from some guys who had Harvard MBAs. They were very intelligent and had an attractive plan in many regards. However, all 10 of us on the investment committee voted no to the deal because there was no transparency. These deals were worth 8 to 10 figures in total, so there was a lot at stake. But yet the real issue with these very bright guys is they did not get our trust or our money because of our gut feeling that there was a lack of transparency."

Joe further said that when people talked about meeting Sam Walton (Wal-Mart) and Herb Kelleher (Southwest Airlines), they related to them because they were so open. "I tried very hard to talk with people not at them. And I found that it was far better to talk about ideas rather than me or what I did."

> *If you put yourself on a pedestal, make sure everyone else is there first.*
>
> —*Joe Croce*

Address Conflicts of Interest or Biases

There is a technique I referenced in the last chapter, precall (page 164), that applies here as well. When you tell people up front about a potential bias, you give them the ability to decide how to weight the value of what you say against that bias. Chances are they will listen objectively. But if you keep quiet and let them uncover your bias on their own later, you risk everything you say being perceived as suspect.

Speak No Evil

A lot of time is wasted because people get negative during communication. As I mentioned earlier, one of the founders of Google, Sergey Brin, used the guiding phrase, "Do no evil" to underscore the need to treat customers with high moral regard. In my work with Harry, I have observed that he follows a similar rule about communication: Speak no evil.

There was an activist in Boston who hired YES to help him do a lot of good work to reach at-risk youth in Boston. However, this man had as part of his agenda his own personal gain and became bogged down and could not pay his bills. This left YES being owed $20,000 during a tight fiscal period.

When this came to light in a board meeting, there were several people who had knowledge of the situation who made it clear that the debtor had revealed some major character flaws. Anger was expressed, but Harry refused to say anything negative about this man. I thought it was interesting because I know Harry was deeply wounded by this man breaking his trust. It was not so much the money but there were other promises and issues involved and Harry was deeply hurt by this man and angry about the betrayal, but he refused to vent that anger. Instead he moved us to invest our time in the next agenda item, choosing to be productive.

> ### *Customers get to vent; leaders don't!*

Keep It Positive

There is a cost associated with allowing communication to become negative:

- Because human beings are emotional, getting negative tends to invite tangents that vent emotions and waste time. Don't get me wrong; venting in some circumstances can be warranted. But as a leader, logic should take you there, not emotions.
- When people get negative, they often move away from talking about ideas and solutions and move to stress-induced talk about people.
- You may appear to be judgmental and people may begin to shut down around you or be less candid.

When there is need to bring up the negative, always focus on the negative as it relates to consequences and costs. Avoid discussing negatives about people except when alone with that individual.

Here are some tips for dealing with negativity or bringing up a negative issue or situation:

- Change a negative statement into an open-ended question that raises the issue. Avoid yes/no questions.
- Focus on facts. Avoid judging motives.
- Avoid talking behind people's backs. Some people don't have the skills or courage to address things in front of the person who is the supposed problem, so they come to you. As a leader, you are elevating the level of discourse when you force people to address issues directly with one another. You may need to bring two people together and get out of the middle. It is better to force uncomfortable candor than to foster rumor. However, there are other occasions when you may need to be the arbiter between those people. When that is the case, don't let much time pass before you step in. When too much time elapses, emotions have a way of making things worse.

Pent-Up Resistance or Negativity in Meetings

Many leaders face a dicey situation when it comes to communicating about change. There are often people who have an entirely negative view of a topic that you need to discuss at a meeting. Here are some options for dealing with another's negativity in order to keep meetings brief:

- If there is a subgroup of people who will be in a meeting that you know are far more negative or emotional about something, consider meeting with them separately as individuals or a group prior to the larger group meeting. Sometimes people just need to be heard and then they can accept and even embrace things they don't like. At the very least, it will likely keep from wasting the time of the larger group. It will prevent you from being in the awkward place of dealing with negativity in front of a larger group.

■ Precall specific items that you feel may erupt into wasted time by setting aside time later or at the end of the meeting for those items. You may want to indicate that certain things can't be addressed "here." But you probably need to create the opportunity for them to be addressed outside of that discussion.

Less Is More

The city where YES is headquartered, Chesapeake, Virginia, offered a 99-year lease on a building that was particularly well suited for the relocation of YES's main facilities. The price was right at $10 per year. YES's reputation made it the top contender for this community space. The only catch was that YES had to take care of funding significant renovation work. Of particular concern was the exterior of the building. The city was rehabbing the area around the building and a new housing neighborhood was being built across the street. Overall, the financial benefit to YES was significant enough to cause us to engage in this project.

During a City Housing Authority meeting to set the terms of the contract, a council member expressed concern that YES had no experience overseeing a construction project of this magnitude.

Harry responded politely and nondefensively by stating that YES had no experience, but that "we would engage the right people to assist us." He quickly finished by adding "we would be glad to have YES address that concern in more depth." There was no attempt to minimize this concern or expound beyond that. It was a legitimate concern and an admitted weakness of the organization in this context.

Harry's lack of defensiveness and resistance of the temptation to try to reduce the validity of this man's point spoke volumes for Harry's credibility. This response, while brief, was in stark contrast to Harry's detailed presentation up to this point. He had been talking about the YES mission and the plans for the use of the building. He was organized and conveyed some very good information, but when it came to this unanticipated question, he subscribed to the old adage that "less is more."

In spite of this weakness, the board voted that night to give YES the lease. I later engaged the council member who raised the issue in conversation. He indicated that given the credible way Harry had conducted himself, he trusted YES to deliver on the promise to finish the exterior in time.

Don't Let Surprises Make You Ramble

I have seen many other leaders in the situation Harry was in cave to the pressure and try to create an argument or justification for some new issue they were not prepared to address. High-trust leaders have no problem saying: "You have a valid point" or "I don't know and I will get back to you." Interestingly, they look smarter when they do so.

It Is Always about Relationships

When it comes to getting things done, Harry frequently says, "at the end of the day, it is always about the relationship." Building strong relationships in this fast-paced world is the central theme on which all these ideas and principles are centered. By now, I think you will agree that the other leaders we discussed are similar to Harry in that they are people we would want as partners. Communication Trust yields successful partnerships and successful partnerships create profit.

Harry's Most Powerful Message

In the years I have been working with Harry, I have never heard him talk about his many accomplishments or many sacrifices. I have learned things about him through accidental discovery. For example:

- I found out that Harry had opened his home to a former drug dealer who was trying to break away from his past life. I then learned that this was one of many young men to whom Harry has given shelter. Some stole from him, but he was not deterred from continuing this practice. But you would never hear Harry reveal this.
- He personally financed YES in the early days. He never would reveal this either.
- He used to get paid to go to the Market for International Programs in Cannes, France, every year to watch movies when he was a programming executive shopping for shows. He had a lifestyle that some would call glamorous. He would not mention this either. Nor would he mention all that he appears to have given up in exchange to follow his calling to serve young people.
- His Harvard MBA and work in Hollywood put him in circles of major names that he could drop, but you would never hear him do that.

> *When leaders with character communicate, people hear conviction.*

As I wrap up this part on Communication Trust, let me come full circle to where we began: character. Harry is a living testament to the power of character to impact other people. I have learned from Harry that the greatest benefit to being humble is what it does to your own psyche or spirit enabling you to mold the strength of your convictions and give you confidence to communicate from a place of tremendous strength. Contrary to popular opinion, humility is a sign of strength and the precursor to the kind of courage that inspires talented people to want to partner with you. You will see more of this in our next competency, Loyalty Trust.

PART V

Loyalty Trust
(How They Feel)

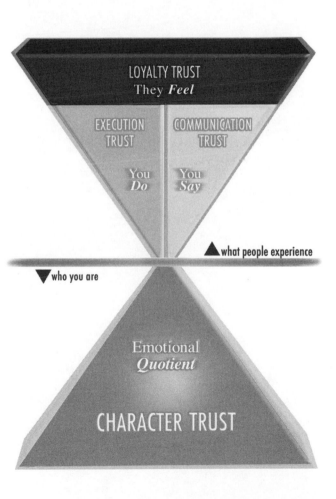

23 | Loyalty Trust Generates Innovation

We have reached the top of the trust model where your hard work to master these competencies turns into a multiplier for you and the success of others. In the first three competencies—Character, Execution, and Communication—we needed to focus on *how* you build each of these critical kinds of trust. As a result of your mastery of these competencies, you earn Loyalty Trust from others that will accelerate your success as a leader.

If you have loyalty, people execute faster, communicate more openly, are more vulnerable, are more receptive to your input, and put forth a much higher level of effort. Money will buy a low to moderate level of loyalty. And if an employee feels dependent on a job, the fear of losing that job will also garner a minimal level of loyalty.

But, having Loyalty Trust is more powerful and cheaper than any other method for motivating people. It frees up enormous time and energy to focus on strategic issues rather than on people problems and that turns into higher profits.

This last part of the book is a bit different from earlier competencies. As with the previous parts, I will give you a few more case studies and practical ideas. Then I will give you ideas on how you may want to use Loyalty Trust to solve generational and diversity problems by teaching others these competencies. And then some final thoughts will tie things together and compel you to take full advantage of the platform Radical Trust will build.

Replacing a Great Leader

After providing a keynote speech at CCG Systems's annual customer conference, Pam asked me if I would work with her company in a consulting capacity. Pam shared that she was getting ready to sell her company to her employees. She wanted me to help develop her leaders to prepare for her retirement.

During my initial coaching sessions as we were discussing leadership traits that Pam brought to the table, several people shared the same insight with me that the president, Nina McCoy voiced, "Pam is like a drug. After time with her, people are on a high. And when they don't get time with her, it is like they are in withdrawal."

You have seen how the leaders we've profiled are very in touch with their people. You could say they have a high level of personal rapport. Whether you work for a large corporation like GAP, a medium-size company like CiCi's Pizza, a small business like CCG Systems, or a nonprofit or government agency like Harry's YES, personal rapport stimulates innovation for a host of reasons. When I say rapport, I am referencing the kind of rapport that comes from caring about people and their future.

This generates a bond with people that is very powerful in business and in life. I'll share specific steps of how great leaders build strong bonds with their people. But first I want to show you an example of how an unusually high level of innovation results from this type of bond.

Loyalty Trust Fuels Innovation

Like many technology companies, CCG Systems's customers rely heavily on an on-going support relationship. CCG has made excellence with support a hallmark of their business. Customers rave about the quality and responsiveness of their support. Allan Richardson is CCG's lead salesperson and he says that, "Without our support staff, there would be no new sales." Allan speaks often of how the support staff's reputation opens doors and closes deals.

In my role as a consultant, I have attended a number of their customer conferences. Their customers have an evangelistic fervor similar to Apple Computer enthusiasts. CCG's customers act as ambassadors. They host prospects at their facilities to demo software and frequently participate in product demonstrations via conference calls to add testimony and validation. The feedback is very consistent that CCG's support is the most responsive and friendliest they have ever experienced with any technology company.

There are several extremely innovative aspects to CCG's approach to customer service that hinge on the high level of trust that exists in the culture. The first is that they rarely fail to uphold their standard of a human answering the phone in less than three rings. Amazingly, in this age of long customer hold times, CCG also has no queue. There is no real hold-time except the few seconds it takes to transfer a call.

Tech industry folks are also amazed when they hear that there are no tiered levels of support at CCG. In the vast majority of technology companies, after a healthy hold-time listening to avant-garde music, you are screened by an inexperienced, lower paid employee. This person may resolve minor problems, but in many cases he acts more as a receptionist who directs your call on to a more advanced level of technical support with more hold time while you are sedated by more music. Or worse, the level-one tech submits a problem report and then reads you the policy that you will be contacted in some amount of time if the problem is not resolved.

At CCG, an extraordinary level of support is delivered by one group of people who work as an incredibly knowledgeable and unified team to solve all customer issues. There is one more thing that makes this support so impressive. There is regular and purposeful turnover on this team. CCG has found that employees who buy into the support culture are great candidates for fueling other talent needs as CCG grows. While there are key members of the support team who love what they do and act as an anchor of knowledge and stability, some members move into other roles in the company, requiring the team to groom yet another new member.

Innovation at All Levels

There is a tendency for many organizations to assume that innovation is what certain people do in certain parts of the company. For example, tradition has it that an ad designer in the marketing department would be an innovator. But the person handling customer calls in support would be a policy-keeping worker bee instead of being an innovator.

This myth is shattered by a company like CCG Systems. As you walk from Wendy's office in marketing where she is eagerly developing a new web site and climb the steps up a floor and pass Brad who is deeply engaged on a support call, you see people innovating as part of their normal course. CCG has far fewer policies and far more innovation. The reason they can do this is because of the extraordinary Loyalty Trust that exists throughout the organization.

Pam has a very flat organization where she is the primary catalyst or leader. She is rare in that she maintains a very high degree of Loyalty Trust with most of the people in her company. However, it was not possible for Steve to keep the same level of loyalty with the thousands of people in his GAP Zone. He had to pick key talent with whom he spent more time. And his loyalty multiplied out through them to others. Given the size and geographic reach of Joe and Harry's organizations, they are like Steve. They are inspiring a high Loyalty Trust among a smaller number of people.

As I share what Pam does to spread Loyalty Trust, remember you may need to do this on a smaller scale.

Five Points Every Leader Needs to Understand to Support Innovation

Point One: *When a leader fosters trust among people, innovation is more natural and the ability to have strategy bubble up from those most intimately involved with the customer is not only possible, it is very productive.*

To give you an example of this, about a year ago I was involved in a support team meeting. Significant projected company growth was fueling strategic discussion about how the team would handle increased support calls. They were trying to figure out how to handle the increased load while also taking calls generated by a new software release.

The idea of going to a tiered tech support department came up. One of the more experienced team members, Bob Auger said, "Wait a minute. That is not loving the customer! Our personal touch is critical to our success. And tiered support usually becomes impersonal." It was clear that tiered support would have made these people's jobs easier in the short term and would have solved the immediate needs. However, this team was invested in the long term and that focus caused the team to quickly agree with Bob and once again resist the temptation for a quick fix.

What is interesting to me is that I don't hear too many people in meetings use words like "loving the customer" and authentically mean it. As I later shared with Bob, it was particularly contrasting since Bob is six feet tall and carries his weight like a linebacker. He is the last person who would be pretentious or mince words. As a hobby that generates extra income, Bob works in management with a security company on weekends. He provides security for Broadway shows, night clubs, and concerts around the country.

Point Two: *Authentic leaders help create a warm environment.*

I am not criticizing companies that have tiered tech support. In many if not most cases, tiered tech support is the right answer and helpful to both the customer and the bottom-line. But I have found that some managers allow the tiers or silos of support to be cold, indifferent, and poorly integrated. Their culture doesn't deal with the fact that the customer is often falling into gaps between those tiers. And the root issue is that, like the employee, the customer is viewed as a cog in the process of making a profit. The real issue with tech support is the same as the struggle every business contends with related to quality. Excellence in processes is hard to maintain as volume increases. High volume tends to cause people to gravitate to a cold, "get-it done" mentality that increases error rates and/or rudeness (from the customer's perspective).

Leaders set the stage for the ultimate tone set toward the customer. As with the other leaders, Pam puts great effort into coaching her people to keep their focus genuinely on the customer. Bob exemplified this with his comments. In fact, he even cited Pam: "The way Pam defines service means that 'every solution we implement must first benefit the customer and never compromise our level of service toward them.' For us, tiered tech support will cost the customer."

There was a pretty tough debate, but Bob and his peers made the right choice to take the harder road that requires a stronger culture. And a big part of the reason is the loyalty they feel to the customer and to Pam's vision for a personal touch with clients. It is important to note that Pam does not micromanage. She gives people great latitude.

She was not at this meeting and probably didn't even know the debate took place. The thing that will draw Pam to get involved is when a situation reveals that someone somewhere in the company didn't properly value the customer or if one of the key character traits we have been discussing is broken. This is her trigger to take someone aside to mentor them related to what she perceives to be a faulty paradigm.

Pam realizes people's paradigms shape the warmth and effectiveness of a culture. She is very good at keeping her finger on the pulse of people's paradigms or thinking. By dealing at that deeper level, she is able to give people wide freedom to do as they see fit.

Point Three: *Clarity of mission combined with high character reduces the need for rules and increases the opportunity for people to innovate.*

Pam is very careful with processes and procedures. She realizes too many rules can stifle creativity. More importantly, she realizes that cultures with lower emotional maturity or character require far more innovation-stifling rules and procedures to govern people to do their best work. CCG Systems, in their hiring, and Pam, in her mentoring, focus on character so they can have minimal rules and maximum innovation.

CCG's cooperation levels are so high that employees feel very comfortable being creative. There are minimal work boundaries. And as a result there is a lot of cross-team functionality. People from different teams work very productively with each other because their loyalty is not to a certain team, but to the customer. Questions you will hear around CCG frequently and sincerely are: "Is this the best and highest use of my talents?" and "Is this really benefiting the customer?"

Point Four: *An atmosphere that requires innovation, needs leaders who can engage people fully and authentically.*

The culture at CCG fosters engagement. These people are true partners. Call-centers, like so many businesses, often do not have cultures that are engaging and thriving. And, therefore, the atmosphere is colder. You may have been surprised how the leaders I quoted in this book expressed a dislike for many of the motivational tricks and rewards that are popular today.

CCG managers don't need to waste time or resources on a lot of team-building stuff that is standard at other companies doing similar work. There is no employee of the month, no spiffs to keep people alert or engaged, no ice-breakers necessary at meetings. The reason is that the warmth of their culture replaces the need for it. I am not knocking team-building, but some team building activities are a feeble substitute for a healthy culture. And some of the distraction of fun and games actually gives weak managers the ability to appear like they are leading.

Point Five: *Innovation is more likely if employees feel like family.*

The bond between a Radical Trust leader and the employees extends beyond commitment to the individual leader and attaches to the values, mission, and vision of the leader's organization and beyond it to its stakeholders. Employees from CCG Systems, CiCi's Pizza, GAP, and YES frequently use the word family to illustrate their feelings toward their constituents.

Andrea Paxton is a technical support specialist who just joined CCG support. She had been a CCG customer when she worked at Texas A&M University's Transportation Services Department.

Pam is very careful not to cherry-pick talent from her customers and always asks them for approval before she will permit a customer to transfer "from one side of the family to the other." There are many other employees of CCG that migrated from being a customer because they loved the culture at CCG.

Andrea told me the following:

> While in college, I did research on great companies to work for and decided I wanted to work for an airline. I chose Southwest because of the family spirit and wonderful culture. But things didn't work out with getting the job I wanted in the right city. But the interviews confirmed how powerful the culture at Southwest was and I wanted to work with a company like that. CCG is the Southwest of the technology world in that it is like a family.
>
> When I was at Texas A&M and a customer of CCG, I could not believe that there was still a technology company that was just a phone call away and that I got a human being who knew what they were talking about. And the fact that I got a person after the first or second ring was incredible.
>
> They genuinely care about customers. Now that I am here, I know my instinct was right. They care about internal folks as well. They treat everyone like family. When I was a customer, I thought they were a very innovative company and so easy to do business with. Now I understand more fully why.

Developing Talent to Innovate by Removing Obstacles

Each one of these leaders practices a bluntness or candor that is received productively because loyalty is established. These leaders have realized that their ability to free talent to soar requires them to be able to help people identify and remove self-imposed obstacles.

Pam once said to me:

> Seeing the strengths of talented people is easy. Helping them chip down to the diamond is the tough part. People need a "truth teller." Without assistance, I would have used far fewer of the talents that I have. And I want to be able to help others release their talents because leaders have done the same for me. I want to spend time with people who want to build people up. It is easy to tear people down. There are too many critics. There are ups and downs in life. I want to be around people who are willing to push each other and if necessary for a season carry each other.

I asked Pam to explain why she so often uses the word love in a business setting. She said, "I believe it has been a focus for much of my business life, and I have grown to recognize more fully just how critical it is for a person to first feel 'safe' (loved) before they can actually be open to receiving direction."

Pam, Steve, Joe, and Harry have created cultures where people feel loved because they understand that functional love is first and foremost about being honest with people.

Loyalty generated through trust transcends silos, borders, and even traditional boundaries between employees, customers, and vendors and raises the quality of relationships in such a powerful way that innovation, quality, and financials are deeply impacted.

24 | With Trust, Firing Can Invigorate a Culture

It may seem odd to share ideas about firing people in the context of discussing Loyalty Trust. But the very reason firing is so hard on everyone is so many managers have not mastered the competencies illustrated in this book. The sum total of the insights in this book have already revealed how Radical Trust can take one of the most difficult jobs a manager faces and make it a more compassionate process.

In fact, you probably find it easy to believe that these Radical Trust leaders have to fire fewer people because their trust-building capability equips them to grow and prosper talent. Too many managers have to depend on the hiring and firing process to let them rotate through talent until they get "lucky." There should be no surprises when it comes to a manager informing an employee that he or she must end the work relationship.

> *Firing is an act of loyalty.*

Firing is also critical to the entire process of building Loyalty Trust with all stakeholders. It is disloyal to everyone, especially the employee, to keep someone who is not a good fit. As a person who has been fired himself, I say this with all due respect and sobriety about the short-term pain employees feel when firing must occur.

> *The goal of hiring and firing is not to populate our culture with people we like, but to populate it with people who share common values and who bring unique talents.*

One of the transformations that is taking place right now in organizations is the increased emphasis on finding and developing talent and on releasing talent that does not fit. In the past, firing someone was far less likely and, in most cases, had more negative impact than it does today. Firing may not mean that a person is a poor performer or is without talent. More likely it means that the person did not have or could not bring to bear the talent needed for that work or their value system did not align with the organization's.

CCG Systems uses the term "counseled out" as a way of underscoring their deep commitment to people, even those that are disengaging from the day-to-day relationship. Pam's approach to what others call firing builds tremendous loyalty from current employees and even the ones she "counsels out."

Over the years, I have witnessed numerous people being counseled out at CCG. In every case, the people continued making contributions up to the end of their time on the payroll. They left with clarity as to why it had occurred and in almost every case an eagerness to move on and build on what they had learned from the experience at CCG. In fact, because Pam pushes such a high level of candor, people counsel themselves out.

Some might argue that Pam has a unique advantage because she is running a small business. Many think that it is easier to maintain productive hiring and firing practices in a small business. Rather than debate that point, I will jump back to Steve and the large corporate setting at GAP to provide some important hiring and firing ideas. I will also pull from a unique government example as well. Although I don't have space to cover all aspects of hiring and firing in this book, I do want to reveal some key aspects of hiring and firing that impact Loyalty Trust.

Hiring and Firing Should Be Part of Any Manager's Role

Hiring needs to be pushed down to the level where the manager who will be the employee's direct report has a key say in the hiring decision. The argument that some of the lower-level supervisors aren't experienced or mature enough to have much of a say in hiring is nonsense. If a supervisor is not capable of participating in hiring, he or she should not be supervising people. In fact, some organizations undermine the development of healthy loyalty by not having managers or supervisors fully involved in the process.

Another abdication of leadership is when senior managers say, "I'm too busy to be deeply involved in the hiring process."

I had the pleasure of working with some Allied Signal managers prior to their merger with Honeywell. In the 1990s, their CEO, Larry Bossidy, helped lead them to increase the return for shareholders by a factor of eight, more than double their operating margins, to 15 percent, and almost tripled their return on equity from 10 percent to almost 30 percent. He was named CEO of the year in 1998. He and business consultant, Ram Charan, authored the best-selling book, *Execution: The Discipline of Getting Things Done* (New York: Crown Business, 2002). Larry said, "The job no leader should delegate—having the right people in the right place" (p. 109).

The interviewing process gives a manager the opportunity to establish clarity about expectations for the relationship. Here is an example from one of Steve's hiring successes, District Manager Christian Kerby, that reveals how building Loyalty Trust should start even prior to hiring—during the interview process:

> Steve, I want you to know that I will never forget our first meeting. You grilled me for two hours . . . and at the end I was so motivated and determined to be on YOUR team. . . . You told me that you saw a spark in me and I had a quality that you were looking for. For that meeting and that interaction, I am forever grateful. I feel that you have given me the appropriate amount of guidance and mentorship to help me grow my career. I look forward to our paths crossing again in the future. I wish you and your family much happiness.

Hiring is a time to set in place a foundation for trust. Firing is part of the critical pruning all people and organizations need and deserve. There are far too many corporations, government agencies, and educational institutions that are enabling poor performance by letting people hide behind policies and procedures that centralize hiring and limit firing. This practice undermines the establishment of strong trust and creates dysfunction.

Partnering with Human Resources

Effective leaders use the advice and processes that are developed and monitored by human resource departments to improve the hiring of talent; but most leaders find that their direct involvement in interviewing the candidate is the key to identifying if the person possesses the talent they want. Many leaders effectively delegate to human resources or other managers some steps in the process, such as screening applicant's resumes and conducting screening interviews.

Most effective human resources executives I know agree that human resources should not drive the hiring process or hiring decision because they do not drive execution. The manager doing the hiring is responsible for execution and therefore should be trusted to manage the front end of execution—hiring talent.

Firing Can Be Compassionate and Productive

When a high-trust leader fires someone, the employee should know it is coming and usually understands and agrees with the decision. And, more importantly, there is no victim because the employee feels he or she has been treated fairly.

Even though firing is common in many organizations, it is rare in education and government. Unfortunately, there are also corporations that have overly centralized or cumbersome processes that prevent managers from exercising proper discretion in firing employees.

If you are a manager in one of these organizations, I understand that this section may not appear to be relevant; however, if you think you don't have the ability to challenge people in a productive way, you should at least ask for clarity on what you can do. You will be surprised how many human resource departments and senior managers are willing to support you in producing accountability.

Many managers assume, incorrectly, that they can't challenge problem employees. Let me give you an example of a leader who came into a position where he did not have firing capability. This is surprising to many because there is a false assumption that in government you just can't fire people. This story disproves that myth and shows just how firing strengthens trust in government or any organization.

I have participated with Sarasota County government's extensive leadership development efforts by providing speeches and training on leadership. Jim Ley, the Sarasota County administrator, has a unique approach to leadership in government, particularly as it relates to firing.

Helping Underperformers Move to a Better Fit

Soon after taking office, Jim asked the County Board of Supervisors to turn all managers into "at-will" employees. This meant that if he could not get managers to commit to excellence, they could be moved to a new position where they would be successful or fired. The board approved Jim's request. He got it because they trusted him and because he was in the early honeymoon phase of his time there.

He was very candid with them about "what it was and was not." It was not about firing people immediately. They knew he was asking for their trust in helping his people operate at their best. They also knew there might be some who were a wrong fit and it would be right and good to be able to help them move on. They also realized that current employees and taxpayers deserved the best managers the county could give them. Over the next year, they saw that the freedom to fire was used effectively. Jim further said:

> This helped our managers to also understand that they must hold their people accountable. One of the critical competencies of a manager is to evaluate and hold others accountable for performance. So it made sense that they be held accountable for their performance as a manager.
>
> We had a problem previously in that evaluating people used to be just paperwork. Too many managers did not take their role to develop people seriously. The ability to fire created opportunity points

and pressures that caused them to act. They started to see people deal with nonperformers and people got excited in a good way.

Many of the managers had previously been put in positions where they were likely to fail and the old message was that was okay. Now, we gave underdeveloped managers the opportunity to develop competencies. And having a culture where managers are required to be better managers made a big difference to our employees.

As would be expected, the ones who were "dealt-with" screamed about a lack of trust. But that was only a few people. The truth was that the ability to fire dramatically improved trust.

The ability to fire managers made it clear that personal responsibility was important. And this was true for our relationship with our unions as well.

It is interesting to note how some of Jim's key leaders view this county's unique approach to accountability and how their new approach to partnering impacted the team spirit and results. Fire Chief Brian Gorski observed:

Through teamwork and the understanding that forming relationships is the key to community outcomes, Sarasota Emergency Services can proudly point to one outcome that means something personally to each of those who it so served. The survivability rate, that is, walking out the front door of the hospital, for cardiac patients who require resuscitation by a paramedic is approaching 30 percent. That rate is 5 percent nationally. Working as a team internally and externally with our emergency room staff, focusing on the same goal, trusting in each other, makes this possible.

Chief Financial Officer Gail Miller links Jim's new approach to financial outcomes:

Working as a team with a strong foundation of trust, we have been able to take an enterprise view of our responsibilities. The old issues of "territory" go away. We stay focused on the outcome and key performance measures. The result is that we have controlled the cost of government per capita growth to be equal to or less than inflation, while absorbing new services, state mandates, and increased health and other personnel costs.

In summary, Sarasota County government's willingness to break away from past tradition became a huge success. In my work with this group, I have noted a vitality that is rare in government organizations. I have interacted with managers from just about every corner of that county and can personally attest to their commitment to both their employees and their taxpayers. In fact, I would bet that, if you met Sarasota County's managers, you would come to the conclusion pretty quickly that this is a group of very talented professionals who are pursuing excellence. The ability to fire people has been an important part of creating a high-trust culture that executes well.

Firing Is a Productive Part of Life

> *If there is trust in the relationship, firing is no surprise, is far less painful, and often is embraced as a good thing.*

Steve once had a district manager who did not possess the talent to fulfill her role. He called her to schedule a time to communicate this assessment in a dignified and compassionate way. When he asked to have some time with her, she said, "I don't think that will be necessary. Didn't you get my e-mail?" Literally as Steve was on the phone, the e-mail appeared in his inbox saying she had resigned.

Steve pointed out that they were on the same page. There was no surprise. She knew what was expected of her, she knew she was not delivering that and, because of Steve's commitment to her success, she knew he had done what he could do to support her success. There were no hard feelings. Steve took the time to reinforce the talent he saw in her and encouraged her that there was going to be a career for her in a different company that had different talent needs. She expressed her full appreciation that Steve was a committed partner.

The key to Steve being 90 percent successful with his hiring and his ability to make firing a less painful process is tied first and foremost to the Loyalty Trust generated by the timing, transparency, and immediacy of his feedback.

25

Trust Is the Bridge to Generational Differences

Pam Nelson often reminds people that, "You don't have to like people to love them." She uses this to challenge her employees to set aside personality and focus on the customer. Or another way Pam says this is, "Focus on potential; not differences." It is interesting to note that CCG Systems, like many organizations, has among its employees a sampling of every generation. And there is no tension or obstacle created by generational differences. In fact, the different points of view that are evident among different age groups are meshed together in a way that yields better innovation and outcomes. However, there are many people who cite that generational differences are a major issue in today's workforce.

I am going to state a heresy in the training and development field: Generational differences are not a disruptive business problem. Let me qualify that statement by adding *if you work in a place that has Loyalty Trust.* I have repeatedly found that the real answer to dealing with generational differences is one of trust. Or another way of saying this is that when some managers can't build the right kind of working relationships with their people, they blame generation differences.

For example, it bothers some managers that the younger generation's loyalty is often not bought with money. Some managers speak with frustration when they claim, "We pay them well. You would think they would have some loyalty to the company." But as we established earlier, more and more people have less faith and dependency on corporations. This bugs some people who grew up at a time when people were taught to "be loyal to your company." What they miss is that many talented people attach loyalty to people not things or organizations.

The real issue with generational differences is that if you focus too much on what you perceive to be the problem, you fail to see the solution. Here is the deeper reality and the good news. Regardless of generation, people respond to the character traits we have been discussing that are central to Radical Trust leadership. That is why at CCG Systems, CiCi's Pizza, the GAP, and YES, loyalty to each other eclipses generational differences. And in every case, multiple generations are present. In the case of GAP and YES, their business centers on dealing with fundamental generational differences that are occurring in fashion for the GAP and in media for YES. There are very few things beyond fashion and music where you will find more generational differences.

I use the same content that I teach business executives about Communication Trust when I have classes for teenage hip-hop artists at YES. The reason why it works with corporate executives and young artists alike is simple: How and why people trust has not changed in thousands of years. The only thing that has changed, as I mentioned earlier, is that more people have the economic freedom to act on that trust. There certainly are huge generational differences, but trust acts as a bridge to allow people to work together effectively. And leaders who have the resulting loyalty are not slowed down by the differences.

> **All generations respond better when engaged as a partner.**

A lot of time is invested in training managers to understand generational differences. This would be fine if the real problem were the differences. But the differences are actually a strength when trust is present. What is really going on in a lot of the cases is that generational differences have become the scapegoat for what is really a trust deficit.

Throughout history, we have examples of people being able to overcome differences to be able to work productively together. Rarely was the primary solution that the leaders involved immersed themselves in understanding why they were different. The real answer came when they either created fear that forced people to work together or they were able to get people to share common values that pulled them together in spite of deep and varied differences.

That is what the leaders profiled in this book have done by mastering these competencies. They have taken values that are appreciated and respected by most anybody and integrated them into the way they lead. The result is a radical bond that overcomes just about everything, including generational differences.

A lot of what is labeled as generational training is bigotry. It is counterproductive and even insulting to lump people into categories by age. Yet, every day in countless training sessions, managers are subjected to this practice of stereotyping. Do you know why this stuff sells? Because it allows people to blame their pain on something.

Focus on building competencies that shape actions and words. Any manager willing to learn and grow can build a trust that all generations respond to. As a result of trust, people let down their guard and managers and employees come to understand the people behind the generational label and value and appreciate each other.

26 | Diversity Is Not the Problem

The global economy has rapidly increased the diversity of the workplace. And many organizations and managers are being challenged to change the way they lead in order to cope. As I proved earlier, that is one of the underlying reasons these competencies are so critical today. I think you will agree that leaders who achieve Loyalty Trust are well situated to be able to manage in diverse environments.

I was in Bangkok recently speaking at Marriott's Asian Pacific General Manager's conference. These leaders found that my trust model and related competencies supported and advanced their already rich history as a Radical Trust organization. Of particular note was how many managers from so many diverse cultures expressed that the character traits critical to execution and communications are universal.

Much attention has been focused on tolerance, as the fundamental solution to diversity. And as a result, political correctness has created the false impression that organizations and leaders should be more tolerant across the board to make the work place more harmonious. In some organizations, this has undermined the fact that trust requires a high level of rigidity with the key foundational character traits that lead to Loyalty Trust.

Where this can be seen vividly is what happened at Enron. Internal honesty and candor became traits that were subjected to relativism and the wrong kind of tolerance undermined the organization. However, the marketplace operates on a more rational and rigorous set of truths and Enron's corporate culture of tolerance for weaker character traits resulted in dire economic and human consequences. Conversely, GAP, CiCi's Pizza, CCG Systems, and YES have had great success because they are intolerant of managers deviating from these character traits.

If you show me a competitive organization with a diverse culture that is successful, I will show you an organization that has managers who have mastered the competencies in this book. Conversely, if you show me a manager who is struggling because he has a diverse workforce, I will show you a manager or culture that has gaps in one or more of these competencies.

As with generational differences, the bridge that unites diverse people is trust. Don't waste your time training your managers on understanding cultural differences until you are sure they are capable of managing in a way that builds trust. Let me use an analogy that is relevant to just about any culture. Trying to solve diversity issues by focusing on understanding differences before you train people how to build trust is like putting the cart before the horse.

27 | Final Thoughts

Many managers have tremendous discipline that is fueled by personal ambition and inner drive. However, discipline for the leaders in this book is energized by something more. Their commitment to people is an equal or greater catalyst for discipline. I say this because one of the misconceptions of discipline is that it comes only from inside the person.

Loyalty and Community Drive Discipline

It is important to realize that another source that fuels will or discipline is a leader's connection to his or her people. Discipline increases in most people as bonds with others grow. Bonds are created as people develop common values and goals and ultimately Loyalty Trust.

In fact, the rigidity or stubbornness that can come from ego-driven discipline can get in the way of progress. Discipline fueled by strong community tends to create fuller engagement and better innovation.

211

I have had the privilege to get to know the Navy Seal Commander who lead combat operations in Afghanistan. It is interesting to note that even in that demanding field, this leader underscored the importance of being able to navigate between being "directive as an officer and participative as a teammate."

He used the term "old charisma" to describe less effective leaders he has managed who tried to keep their distance and lead from the traditional place of title and authority in an impersonal way. And he underscored that the "old approach" just does not work as well with the current Seals who are "talented, deeply committed, and have lots of career options." Over 75 percent of candidates don't make it through their training program. The Navy, like business, needs to retain these highly trained professionals when it comes time for reenlistment. And in fact they work hard at retention.

He went on to say, "You have to know where a person is coming from. Knowing their values requires a personal connection. That is trickier because you do have to know where to draw the line when you need to command and where to engage at a participative or personal level." There is no doubt that Seals are among the most disciplined professionals in the world and also among the most effective at executing missions. What is so relevant to the message in this book is that, this commander is confirming that the way you communicate with your people impacts both discipline and loyalty. His view is supported not only by his success as a ranking officer, but the fact that Seals refer to themselves as a "community."

Leaders Must Meter Trust

Great leaders work hard to earn trust and also carefully and thoughtfully meter trust to others. By meter I mean that we all earn trust from other people based on our character that is revealed by our execution and communication.

However, it is important to dispel the myth that leaders should give trust freely without insuring people deserve it. It is not a bad thing to require people to earn your trust. The hiring process if done correctly is designed to figure out how much responsibility and freedom an organization can give a person.

This is the fundamental difference between judgment and discernment. Judgment says, "I will not permit you to earn my trust." Discernment permits trust to grow between us. It can be a disservice to give too much trust. As the old saying goes: "Some managers give their people so much rope that they hang themselves." Frankly, freely giving trust can be an excuse for not doing the coaching or mentoring that a manager should do. And conversely, sometimes managers micromanage and refuse to give trust that is deserved. It is very inspiring to earn someone's trust. And it is gratifying to give it when earned.

Pride Can Be Dangerous

Every leader in this book voiced the danger of pride in reducing trust and crippling leadership:

> Steve said, "It is good to be proud of your people, but dangerous to have pride in yourself."
>
> Joe said, "You have to become deaf as you become successful. You have to be careful because if you start internalizing all the accolades you get, you can destroy your ability to connect with people."
>
> Harry said, "It is illogical to have pride. I am not of my own making."
>
> Pam said, "Pride is dangerous and I have a healthy fear of it."

Gratitude

It has often been said that a spirit of gratitude prevents pride from taking root and is the key to a positive attitude. In my work with these leaders and others like them, I have witnessed that to be true. And each has parts of his or her life story where he or she was down and struggling and had to make a choice to have an attitude of gratitude.

Get Radical

I recommend starting with one of these competencies and going to your people and laying out with candor what you want to work on and what you would like them to work on. Nothing engrains new knowledge like teaching others. Use the examples in this book as teaching tools. And like Ben Franklin, continue to move through these competencies only to start over again to ensure you keep building the bridge to success.

  People are waiting for you!

Index

About the Author

Wall Street Journal writer, Sue Shellenbarger, called Joe a "pioneer and renaissance man whose content is filled with distilled wisdom." Joe's career as an entrepreneur, banker, and the senior executive of three companies provides a strategic and authentic perspective. He brings a rare combination of insight and energy. His experience as CEO of a rapid-growth retail chain ensures that his innovative ideas relate to audiences and readers in a way that is relevant to a busy and competitive marketplace. His hands-on work as a consultant/general manager leading companies as a turnaround expert ensures that Joe's message provides solutions and motivation that have real-world traction. Voted "World's Best Presenter" by journalists in 2000, his unique message and inspiring style have made him a sought-after speaker on change, leadership, and growth. His consulting/speaking practice, which started in 1989, has taken him to Australia, Thailand, Germany, Canada, the UK, New Zealand, and all 50 states.

To invest in character building, Joe, his wife Jill, and their three children moved into a customized motor home. They schooled, worked, and lived together for 18 months as they traveled through

44 states. The benefit this journey reaped for his family proved that the principles Joe teaches to professionals also apply to people's personal lives.

His *pioneering* lifestyle, leadership experience, and award-winning speaking set him apart as an inspiring business speaker who weaves stories that motivate audiences to action and imparts immediately practical solutions. Joe lives in Virginia Beach, Virginia, with his wife, Jill, and three children, Joe, Jen, and Josh. Joe also serves on the board of the at-risk-youth development program, Youth Entertainment Studios.